Praise for *Gold Star Father*:

"Scott Warner should be applauded for having the courage to write such a personally revealing book. The honesty in his story is something all non-fiction writers should aspire to. Gold Star Father provides insight into the pain that a father of a fallen soldier experiences in the aftermath."
— KELLY FARLEY, AUTHOR, *Grieving Dads: To the Brink and Back*

"A book everyone should read."
— C.D. WAGNER, AUTHOR, *the Manufactured Messiah*

"Keep the tissues handy—you're gonna need the whole box!"
— FLOYD JONES, AUTHOR, *Blueberry*

"The author's experience of moving through grief, hope, and recovery is soulful, and I tip my hat to him for having the guts to write this book."
— DENNIS CRAIG, EDITOR, Pro Manuscript Review

"Warner's book brought back shards of memories of when I lost my brother in the Viet Nam War. Grief doesn't change much . . ."
— DWIGHT BARTON, Viet Nam Vet

GOLD
STAR
FATHER

Honoring a Hero—Remembering a Son

Fr Terry,   4/18/18

Such a pleasure to meet
you. Share the message
of transformational grief!

Scott N. Warner

GOLD
STAR
FATHER

Honoring a Hero—Remembering a Son

Scott N. Warner, M.B.A., M.A.P.P.

Warner Inspirational Media
Canton, Ohio

ISBN: 978-1478362951

ISBN: 1478362952

Printed in the United States of America

Dedication

This book is a project of love, pain, and redemption. I couldn't have written it without the support of my wife, Melissa, and my sons Chandler, and Ashton.

Honoring a Hero. Remembering a Son. Pvt. Heath Warner
KIA, Operation Iraqi Freedom
1/2/1987 - 11/22/2006
A Simple Person Who Gave So Much

In addition, I dedicate this book to all families who lost loved ones serving in the military, as well as the brave veterans who are serving in harm's way, or have returned home.

1

Preparing for War

I retied my shoelaces, and chatted with my fellow runners as I waited for the start of the Fireman's 9/11 Tribute 5K Race on September 10, 2006. My hands clenched a flag emblazoned with a photo of my oldest son—*this one's for you, Heath,* I thought as I raised the flag at the starting gun's piercing crack. I took up running a few years earlier to improve my health, but I found it boring, and I detested it—now, it's a favorite pastime. Friends from work persuaded me to run with them, and I began to appreciate the sense of well-being that always follows a run. Entering 5K races helps improve my running times, and now it appeals to my competitive spirit.

This race honored not only the memory of those who perished in terrorist attacks on the United States on September 11, 2001, but also the first responders, and service men and women who protect our country. I entered the race as a tribute to my son, Pvt. Heath Warner, who was in Hawaii preparing to deploy to Iraq the next day. The race was my own little adventure because my wife, Melissa, and my two youngest sons were at home sleeping.

While running is normally my time to pray and think about God, today my mind was on Heath. It was cloudy and cool, and the dismal weather reflected my turbulent state of mind. Tomorrow, my son would join his fellow Marines heading to Iraq to help prevent future violence against the United States.

My thoughts raced. *Will he survive? Will he be physically, or mentally injured? How will he handle the hardships of the desert? Will he be homesick? What will we do if something happens to him? How will our family survive? How will I survive?* I was proud to carry the flag with my son's image, and yet I feared for his future.

As I ran through the community where I spent my childhood, I reminisced about my days growing up in the small town. Many people consider our tightly-knit community an idyllic place to raise children—parents proudly cheer their kids in school plays and sports contests, and the entire town turns out for high school football games. Every year our marching band accompanies a military color guard in the Memorial Day parade, honoring veterans for their service and sacrifice for our country. In today's race, I experienced a renewed appreciation for these veterans—their sacrifices in World War II and other conflicts preserved the safe, and free small-town life I cherish.

When I sprinted past my childhood home, my dad came out and took pictures. I chuckled to myself—my parents were as proud of me as when I was a young child!

Then, a sobering thought. Now one of my own children—their grandchild—was grown up and heading off to war.

As I neared the finish line, I glanced back to see a competitor nipping at my heels. I was determined she wasn't going to pass me, but as we came down the home stretch, she dashed ahead of me, and beat me by a hair. I raised my flag high as I crossed the line for a second-place finish. Far from being disappointed, I was proud to have honored my son.

The result? I was awarded my first-ever medal for placing second in my age group! I decided to place the medal above my desk at work as a constant reminder of Heath's dedication to the Marines.

I couldn't wait to tell Heath, but I had to wait until mid-afternoon EST because of the six-hour time difference between Ohio and Hawaii.

"Hey, Heath, guess what I did this morning?" When he learned I dedicated the race to him, he was pleased, and impressed. We spoke for a few minutes about his departure for Iraq the next day, but that was about it—it didn't dominate our conversation.

Though I was sending Heath to war, I denied death was a possibility. *It will not happen to our family,* I told myself. *It always happens to someone else.* We're a Christian family—and I believed whatever happened, we would pray for God's protection of Heath. He would return home safely.

As we hung up, I recalled Heath's last visit home in August. We anxiously awaited his arrival at the airport for his three-week leave, and we finally spotted him in his civilian clothes, and favorite Pac Sun hat. He didn't look to the right or left, but instead focused on his family as he ran down the hall into our arms. The entire family joined in the hug, without caring what we looked like, or who was watching. Heath was finally home!

But … he wasn't the same Heath. The kindhearted son we sent to Hawaii as a new Marine was now a warrior. He just returned from his pre-deployment training in 29 Palms, California, his mental focus geared for combat. He couldn't relax or sleep, and he wandered the house late at night. Anxiety radiated from him in waves as the knowledge of his departure for Iraq weighed heavily. As his family, we supported him the best we could. We treasured every moment with him, and dreaded the end of his leave. When we dropped him off at the Akron-Canton Airport for his return to Kaneohe Bay, little did we know it would be the last time we would see him alive.

Heath knew for a long time that he would deploy for Iraq in 2006. However, he didn't tell his mother, or me, for some time because he knew we would be distraught. In fact, Heath notified most of his friends by a MySpace posting after his deployment, because he didn't have the heart to hurt his friends with his news:

War!!

Current mood: 😔 *numb*

This is for you who actually will reading this, and it is exactly what you think it is!! Im departing for iraq on the eleventh of september!! It's actually really funny in a really sick and sad way but I wont go there....not this time! but at the same time I did'nt post this up to make you sad or upset...no that was never my intention to hurt you, and You have my sincerest apologies if I did hurt you!! Im not goin to spend the entire time on this though. The bottom line is that I will be there approximately 6+ months I will be in a rotation so to speak around a certain area in which I cannot tell you but think of my deployment as a vacation so to speak. If you want my overseas address please IM me of leave me a message or contact me in any way and I will give it to you!! My email is Driftergfc@yahoo.com. Well I once again apologize if I made you cry or feel hurt, but I promise I'll be back very soon –Heath

After he left for Hawaii, the reality of his pending tour in Iraq became traumatic for our family. Every night we saw reports of more war deaths on the news, and I soon found out no matter how much I thought I could handle it, once the reality hit, my whole world imploded.

We exchanged plenty of texts, phone calls, and emails with Heath as he prepared to deploy for Iraq from his Hawaiian base. He had a special bond with his mom, and they often spent countless hours on the phone, especially on the days preceding his departure. They were best friends, and they talked about everything and anything. His last text to Melissa and me was to thank us for being his parents, to tell us how much he loved us, and he would see us soon.

I had to call him one last time just before he left on September 11, 2006. "I love you," I told him, barely choking out my words.

"I love you too, Dad," he replied, his voice breaking with emotion. It was our last spoken goodbye on the last day his feet proudly stood on American soil.

When Heath left for Iraq, the insurgency was at its zenith, and the daily reports of more casualties from IEDs (improvised explosive devices) burdened my family. We learned the insurgents' technology was on par with America's ability to defend our troops against it. The insurgents' IEDs could pierce the underside of our military vehicles—the vehicles in which Heath would be traveling throughout Iraq.

An IED, also known as a roadside bomb, is a homemade weapon constructed and deployed in ways other than in conventional military action. Constructed of conventional military explosives such as an artillery round, it's detonated by military vehicles driving over it, or by a remote device such as a cell phone. The explosions are always unexpected, devastating, and often deadly.

The political environment was intense at the time Heath deployed, and the war was a central theme in the Presidential election between John Kerry and George W. Bush. Even after losing the election, Kerry continued to display a lukewarm attitude toward the military.

On October 30, 2006, Kerry was a headline speaker at a campaign rally for Democratic

California gubernatorial candidate, Phil Angelides, at Pasadena City College in California. Speaking to an audience comprised mainly of college students, Kerry said, "You know ... education ... if you make the most of it, study hard, do your homework and make an effort to be smart, you can do well. If you don't, you get stuck in Iraq."

As a parent of a son whose fondest dream was to join the Marines, I was outraged. I wrote the following letter to the *Canton Repository*, which was published on November 9, 2006:

Kerry Has Minimized Sacrifices of Troops

Here we go again! John Kerry's comments hit a new low in an already overkill political season. I'm a proud Marine dad, and my son, Heath, is serving in Iraq. My parents raised me around core values of God, family and country. I raised my son with similar values. When the events of 9/11 took place, Heath was a freshman at McKinley High. Heath, like many other young men and women, was significantly impacted by those events. He enlisted in the Marines his senior year because of his deep sense of patriotism and desire to serve the county. It is an honor and a privilege to have a child defend this awesome country we live in. I resent any politician who would intentionally, or unintentionally, make a comment that minimizes the sacrifices our servicemen and servicewomen make. John Kerry's tasteless, reckless statement continues a long line of negative comments against our troops. In my book, Kerry's "apology" is too little too late. SCOTT N. WARNER, CANTON

This heightened political environment only added to my daily worry, and I couldn't escape the Iraq War. It was constantly on my mind, and a sense of dread weighed on me like a wet blanket. Each day dragged on as I hoped and prayed the Marines wouldn't come to our door. I marked off each passing day on my calendar at work, and all I could do was survive each day, holding my breath. I couldn't concentrate or sleep as an ominous fear grew, and time progressed slowly with little communication from Heath.

2

The Unexpected Visit

"Heath made it to Kuwait!" I shouted to Melissa as I read my son's MySpace posting in mid-September. We knew he would soon arrive at his assigned duty in Iraq, and we simply couldn't relax. Though communication from Heath was sporadic over the next few weeks, we eagerly poured over each email message and MySpace posting.

Every time I heard from Heath, my mind kept returning to an incident that occurred shortly before he left home for the last time. It was very late, and he was in his bedroom, crying. Melissa sat with him trying to comfort him, but to no avail. He said he wanted to tell her something, but he couldn't because he didn't want to upset her, so she held him in her arms. She believes he knew he wasn't coming home, and he didn't have the heart to tell her.

Heath randomly walked through the house, opening closet doors and cabinets—just going from room to room.

"Heath, what are you doing?

"I'm just taking it all in, Mom."

He apparently sensed his destiny, and he was preparing to say goodbye in his own way. I envisioned Jesus in the Garden of Gethsemane wrestling with his own pending death, as well as what was ahead for him. Our Lord cried out to God to take this cup away from him, but at the same time stating, *not my will, but Your will be done.*

Melissa sent weekly packages to Heath, and I sent a letter every day—his friends in his unit were jealous. However, Heath shared his Twizzlers and other snacks with them, and Melissa soon earned the nickname "Mom" among his entire unit.

I tried to keep Heath up to date on Ohio State and his high school team, the McKinley Bulldogs—we had season passes, so I took pictures of us at the games, and sent them to him. Heath's brothers, Chandler and Ashton, also sent letters, and he was always in our thoughts. We wanted him to know we missed him.

Even though we tried to continue our daily activities, we were numb and scared.

"I have this awful feeling in my spirit that Heath isn't going to come home alive," I told my mom in early October 2006.

"Honey, I have the same feeling," she admitted. There. I finally expressed my deepest fear aloud, and hearing my mother's confession of the same fear only heightened my anxiety about Heath's safety.

Through October, our contact with Heath was limited, but we did receive one letter from him on October 28, 2006. He told us on his first day in Iraq his vehicle hit an IED, but no one was injured. It was a jolt to all of us the war was real, and Heath was in harm's way.

I prayed for Heath. Because he was in the desert, I saw this as his personal spiritual desert experience. I knew his physical and emotional conditions were challenging, and I prayed for him to meet encouraging Christian friends, because I knew Heath could easily be discouraged without support from his friends and family.

Heath's adjustment to the Marine Corps was challenging—because of his sensitive temperament, he often took the brunt of verbal or physical bullying by other Marines. One day, while Heath's unit was standing in formation, a Marine standing behind him hazed him, so Heath turned around, punched the man squarely in the face, and knocked him out. Then Heath calmly turned back around, picked up his rifle, and returned to formation. The Sergeant stopped at Heath and said, "I wouldn't mess around with you, Warner," and he continued in formation.

God answered my prayers for Heath to find Christian friends who would provide emotional and spiritual support. In his letter, he told us he met two Christian friends, and they were reading *The Purpose-Driven Life* by Rick Warren. Heath and his buddies held bible studies, and they prayed together each day. I found peace in the knowledge his spiritual needs were being met. I knew God was with him on the foreign field in Iraq, and I was praying God would become more real to him during this time, and he would know Him in a deeper way.

Little did I know ...

As October swept into November, my anxious feelings intensified. Other than the one letter, we hadn't heard from him, and Melissa and I worried about his safety.

"Well, Heath made it through another day," I'd say each evening after I got home from work. As time passed with no word from our son, I asked Melissa to stop at the recruiter's station to see if she could find out any information. As it turned out, at work Melissa ran into the Gunny Sergeant from the recruiter's station. He told her to give it another week, and if we hadn't heard from him by then, he would see what he could find out.

Despite the lack of news from Heath, we were determined to follow our favorite Thanksgiving traditions. Thanksgiving is our family's favorite holiday, and Melissa always starts preparing for our Thanksgiving feast the evening before. On Thanksgiving Day, she baked special rolls for the boys as they watched the Macy's parade. We welcomed friends and family for Thanksgiving dinner, nibbled on leftovers throughout the afternoon and, as additional guests arrived, we watched football, played games, and sat in the front room laughing, and talking.

Having Heath overseas for Thanksgiving and Christmas was hard, but we were still looking forward to this special time of year. We packaged his Christmas gifts and sent them to him in early November, so he would receive them in time for Christmas. Melissa, the boys, and I eagerly created gifts that would make Heath feel part of the family celebration, even though he was thousands of miles away. We made a miniature lighted Christmas tree with tiny pictures of each of us, and we wrote messages to him in glitter on a Christmas stocking. To give him a taste of home, we included a DVD of a fireplace with a yuletide log burning while Christmas music played. We packed his favorite candy, Swedish fish, and made sure he was stocked up on practical, much-needed toiletries, socks, t-shirts, and underwear. We knew he would celebrate

Thanksgiving with his Marine unit as we were with our family at home.

On Wednesday, November 22, 2006, Melissa and I dropped the boys off at school, and we were looking forward to our day together. We thought we would miss the evening rush at the store by getting our groceries early, and we wanted the largest turkey we could find. That was a must, since our family and friends would visit throughout the day, and everyone would munch on the leftovers—we knew there wouldn't be anything left.

Spending time with Melissa was fun—we rarely had time alone, so grocery shopping was an enjoyable time together. We carefully selected each item in anticipation of the next day's family gathering. Melissa always made her own dressing from scratch with apple, celery, onion, and seasonings. It slow cooked overnight, and we always awakened on Thanksgiving morning to the delicious aroma of homemade dressing. I made the mashed potatoes, because I knew just the right amount of milk, butter, and salt. Melissa's mother made buttered noodles, which was one of Heath's favorites, and I always made sure there were plenty of rolls. Of course, we rounded out the meal with a traditional homemade pumpkin pie.

As we shopped, our conversation drifted to Heath. Even though he wouldn't be discharged until August 2009, we considered his return home.

"You know, we're going to have to help him work through his PTSD," I told Melissa. She agreed, and we talked about the challenges we, as a family, would have to work through with him. We thought of making a bedroom for him in the basement with its own kitchenette where he could live while he attended college.

We were hopeful and optimistic for his safe return, and we found it easier to think of his coming home, as opposed to thinking about his being in combat in Iraq.

I told Melissa I longed to receive a letter from him to share with our family and friends at our Thanksgiving table, and we couldn't help but wonder how he was holding up.

With our shopping complete, we headed home. We cherished the drive together on this beautiful, rare late fall day with the warm sun reflecting off the trees' golden leaves, our conversation filled with holiday anticipation. Little did we know as we were driving to our home, several Marines in another vehicle were also traveling to our home to meet us. At noon, we pulled into the driveway, and Melissa checked the mailbox.

"No letter, Scott." I was extremely disappointed. I desperately missed Heath, and I needed to hear that he was safe, and doing well.

The Unexpected Visit

I went upstairs for a moment when I heard Melissa screaming outside. I panicked. Sprinting down the stairs, I knew something was terribly wrong, and I thought someone was attacking her. As I reached the bottom step, Melissa was trying to tell me the Marines were at our house. I could barely understand her through her sobbing.

When she first saw them, for a split second she thought Heath was surprising us with a Thanksgiving visit—but she quickly realized Heath wasn't with them.

"Please tell us you are not the mother of Pvt. Heath Warner," one of them said.

Melissa screamed and collapsed, dropping the groceries. It was a scream that only comes from a heart being ripped apart—a scream from deep within her soul.

I couldn't make sense of what was happening as three Marines stood in our front room—my head was spinning, and I was dazed by their presence. One of the Marines calmly asked me to sit down, but I couldn't.

I knew instantly why they were there.

"Is Heath dead?" I asked, as a cold realization swept over me.

"Yes."

Yes. I could barely comprehend.

"Are you sure it's Heath?"

"Yes, sir. He has been identified by a dog tag in his boot, and by his identification card." The Marine handed me a casualty report, which stated the particulars surrounding the events of Heath's death:

Date and Time of Incident: 20061122/0920//
Place of Incident: Haqlaniyah//IZ

Circumstances: Pvt. Warner was killed in action while conducting combat operations against anti-Iraqi forces in the Al Anbar Province. Pvt. Warner was the gunner of a M1114 high mobility multi-purpose wheeled vehicle with Level 1 armor that was struck by an IED. Pvt. Warner was killed instantly by the blast. Pvt. Warner was pronounced deceased at 1030 on 20061122 by LCDR Friedrich, medical physician. The body was identified by LCDR Friedrich, medical physician, by means of identification card. Pvt. Warner was wearing the new Kevlar Helmet, Flak Jacket with two ESAPT Plates, Side SAPI Plates, Ballistic Goggles, Nomex Gloves, throat and groin protectors and Quad Guard Gear. This report was reviewed by LTCOL Gridley, RCT-7, XO, at 3613-505. Unit POC 13 is 2NDLT SMITH, 3614-201.
Inflicting Force: Enemy Forces
Cause of Death: Severe Blast Injuries

The Unexpected Visit

As I read the report, disbelief, numbness, and an unimaginable heart-rending pain gripped my body, mind, and spirit.

I stumbled to a chair.

3

In a Flash

In a flash, our family changed forever, and our worst fear was our new reality. In my heart, I cried out to God in anguish.

"No! You cannot take our son! I can handle anything, but please don't take any of my children." But, it was too late—one of my children was gone.

Melissa and I couldn't stop sobbing, and we tried to make sense of what was happening. All we could do was look at each other.

"What do we do now?" Neither of us had answers.

How do we choose a funeral home? How do we interact with this military world that is so foreign to us? How do we tell Heath's brothers, grandparents, aunts, uncles, and his friends? We knew there was much to do, but we had no idea where to start.

Our Casualty Support Officers had paperwork we needed to complete, and we were left to tell our sons their brother was killed in the war. Ashton was only seven, and Chandler was fourteen—how could we tell them? How could we break our children's hearts, knowing they will enter a level of pain they haven't previously experienced?

We had no choice. We decided to let the boys finish the day, and tell them when they came home from school. In the meantime, I began calling our friends and family, and each call brought its own fresh, unique pain.

My first call was to my good friend and neighbor.

"Heath is dead. Please call our pastor." I choked on my words, and I could barely catch my breath.

Then I called my mother.

"Mom, Heath was killed by an IED today. I need you to come over to the house as soon as possible." Still in her pajamas, she was one of the first to arrive.

Then Dad.

"I need you." He immediately closed the pharmacy, and raced to the house. In tears, my dad kept repeating, "I'm so sorry—I'm so sorry."

Melissa's father was at an electricians' conference when I called, and I had to tell him to find a private spot where he could talk to me.

"Dad, Heath was killed today." Through his tears, he cried over, and over, "No! No! Don't tell me that!" I did my best to remain calm as I asked

Melissa's father to break the news to Melissa's mother—I couldn't face telling her Heath was never coming back.

Time stopped, but we had tasks to complete— we started by picking up Ashton at Worley Elementary. His teacher was a good friend and as we entered the school office, we notified the principal of our loss. The staff members' faces were masks of shock and disbelief, and I'm sure they could tell we were in shock ourselves. I met Ashton, and Melissa went into his classroom to tell his teacher our tragic news.

I'm sure Ashton sensed something was wrong, but we couldn't tell him right away. We drove home as if nothing had happened, asking him how his day went. But as we pulled in the driveway and sat there for few minutes, we knew we had to tell him. The Marines were in the house, and family was arriving.

Melissa took over.

"Honey, we need to talk to you about something before we go into the house."

A look of dread washed over his face.

"We have bad news to tell you ... your brother was killed today in Iraq."

"Is my brother an American Hero?" His response caught me off guard.

"Yes, Honey, your brother is an American Hero," she firmly replied. Because Ashton was so young, we knew he couldn't comprehend our news, so we sat in the car for a few moments, all of us in shock.

With that, we went into the house and began to receive family, friends, and neighbors who came by to share their condolences.

While we were waiting to pick up Chandler from school, we received a phone call from a good friend. Word was spreading through text messaging that Heath was killed, and we knew we had to pick him up right away before he heard the news from someone else.

The principal and guidance counselor met us at the middle school door—the elementary school called the middle school, and prepared them for what was happening. They took us to the nursing station, and we waited for Chandler.

The sounds of an ordinary middle school day surrounded us, students moving through their normal routines. Students arrive, attend classes, eat lunch, attend more classes, and then head for home. The sounds of laughter and slamming locker doors fill the hallways, and it's a place for the innocence of childhood. It's a place for hanging out with friends, joking around, and being silly. I knew when I broke the news to Chandler, school would never be normal for him again. He would be thrust onto a new life path that would be painful, sad and lonely—he would enter into the reality of an adult world.

I dreaded what was ahead.

A few minutes later, Chandler came in. Seeing his mother and father standing before him, he was confused and anxious. When Melissa told him his brother was gone, he began to pound on the wall. We tried to comfort him the best we could, but his heart was broken.

Finally, he settled down, and there was an awkward silence. None of us knew what to do. The guidance counselor tried to be supportive by putting her arm around him, but he didn't want to be touched.

"Dad, I want to stay for wrestling practice." *What? Stay for practice?* I had my doubts because Chandler was so distraught, but I decided to let him go. I told his coach to have him run and, under no circumstances, was he to wrestle. I was concerned Chandler might inadvertently hurt another student because he was so angry.

Shortly after we arrived home, the phone rang, and it was the coach, insisting we pick up Chandler. Contrary to our request, the coach allowed Chandler to wrestle. In his anger, Chandler body-slammed a teammate to the mat hard enough to injure him during a practice wrestling match. When he arrived home, he was still pounding his fists into the wall.

Chandler's anger stayed with him for a long time. Later, he recalled the moment he learned of his brother's death.

"I'll never forget the day my brother died. I woke up and had a normal morning, and my day seemed to be going better than usual. When I was eating breakfast, my mom and I were talking about my brother, Heath, wondering what he was doing, because he was in the United States Marine Corps, and he was in Iraq. I came to school and was having a great day, but little did I know it was going to be my last good day for a very long time. It was the last period of the day, and they called me to the office, so I knew something was going on. The school attendance lady told me to follow her to the nurse's office. I walked in, and saw my Mom and Dad standing there. A few seconds later my Mom said, "Chandler, something terrible happened to your brother. He was killed in Iraq today." To tell you the truth, I can't even remember what I did. I felt numb."

At the age of fourteen, Chandler stepped into the role of eldest son, no longer having a loving older brother to guide his way.

Ashton continued to cling to the vision of Heath as an American hero, and he thought of his brother all the time. Initially, Ashton poured his grief into drawing—in one picture, he drew a grave marker with the inscription:

"Heath Warner, my brother my hero was brave and strong."

I hung the American and Marine Corps flags on the front porch as I had done every day since Heath left, as long as the weather cooperated. The evening sun, shining on the flags like a spotlight, seemed to magnify our loss. I was proud of Heath, his courage, and honor. With friends and family surrounding us, I promised Melissa from that moment on, our son would receive a hero's honor to the utmost we could provide for him.

November 22, 2006, was the most heartbreaking day of our lives.

4

A New Year's Gift

On New Year's Eve, December 31, 1986, I was at a party with about twenty friends from the singles group at my church. We had a great time—plenty of laughter and food made the evening pass quickly. A game of charades was sillier as the night went on, and we were laughing hysterically. My friend, Doug, was there, and his sister, Melissa, was at the hospital in labor with her first child. Could a New Year's baby be born?

At midnight, Doug received a page from her, and everyone was excited because we thought it was the call telling us she was going to have her baby. It was a false alarm, however, and she was calling to wish him a happy New Year—it wasn't until January 2, 1987, that the baby was born.

Doug was her birthing coach, and Melissa's labor was complicated—Heath's delivery was even more challenging. He stopped breathing, and the doctors needed to attach a suction cup to his head in order to bring him into the world.

Heath Douglas Metzger. Although I didn't know it at the time, his birthday would become one of the most important days in my life.

My own entry into the world took place on October 2, 1963, in Canton, Ohio. I grew up in Louisville, Ohio, a small town where everybody knows each other's name, and I came from a family of eight. My dad was an entrepreneur, and he opened his own pharmacy in our community after graduating from Ohio State University. He worked hard to provide for his family, and my mother was a devoted stay-at-home mom.

As a middle class, traditional Italian Catholic family, we attended Mass every Sunday, and visited my grandmother after church. Our family dinners consisted of pasta, and homemade meatballs—it was our Sunday family ritual.

I have a picture of me taken in second grade at my first communion—I was dressed in a white dress shirt, and a navy blue tie. All the boys making first communion were wearing the same uniform for our special day. A crucifix hung in the background, and I was holding a prayer book—as I looked at the camera, I had the most innocent look on my face, and a sweet smile. Over the years, I have come to love that photo—it captured a time before the trials and challenges of adult life wore me down. As an adult, I often look at that picture and wish life could still be simple and sweet.

From early childhood, I felt a deep sense of compassion and empathy, and those traits remain integral aspects of my character. I have sensitivity for hurting and lost people, and as I was growing up my parents were active in prolife causes. I remember thinking, *how can a pregnant woman kill her baby?* Over the years, I developed a strong conviction for life and, as I matured, I was more involved in the prolife movement. However, my deep emotions allowed life's experiences to pierce my spirit and stab my soul, and public school was particularly challenging. Kids picked on me because I was short and shy, I struggled to fit in and to find friends, and I was endlessly searching for acceptance and love that eluded me.

As a teenager, I sought acceptance and love through church, and I believed only God could fill my emptiness. In my early teen years, I devoted myself to the Catholic faith, and I was active in the church youth group. I ran for parish council when I was in high school, joined the Boy Scouts, and I attained the rank of Eagle Scout. Developing leadership skills and stretching myself was important, and I found myself gravitating to organizations where I could increase my skills.

When I was fourteen and working on my Catholic Scouting religious medal, Ad Alteri Dei, one of the church leaders interviewed me, and asked if I knew I were going to Heaven. I struggled with the question, because I honestly didn't know. Although I received the Catholic Sacraments, the interviewer shared with me that having a personal relationship with God is important. That conversation turned my life around because it was then I realized a relationship with Jesus Christ was exactly what I was seeking.

It was also a turning point in my Christian walk. I attended a non-denominational church in my later high school years, but I still attended Mass on Saturday evenings. Between my family, my faith, and my experiences in the Boy Scouts, I developed a love for God in my heart—family, and country became my core guiding principles. Those principles forged the person I was to become and, much later, I instilled the same core values in my own family.

I graduated from Louisville Senior High School in 1982—I left a legacy of Student Council

President, Eagle Scout, and Outstanding Senior runner-up for my class. In 1986, I graduated from Ohio State University with a Bachelor in Science in Business Administration, and that's when I stopped attending the Catholic Church, and I started attending other churches, struggling to find my spiritual path.

After graduation, I returned home and continued to attend the non-denominational church I attended prior to college. I joined its singles group, and I reconnected with Doug who was an old high school friend. Although I was living at home, I was looking for an apartment, and a roommate. As it worked out, Doug's roommate was moving out, and he asked me if I wanted to move in. I looked forward to being on my own again, and I was ecstatic about the prospect of rooming with my old friend.

I knew Doug had a sister, and although we weren't friends at the time, I knew who she was, and I noticed she wasn't attending church. I thought it odd, but she was three years younger than I, so I wrote it off to her "teenageness"—they sometimes stop attending church. It's a time of searching for many teenagers, so I wasn't overly concerned— besides, it wasn't my business.

At a men's retreat, Doug's father addressed the group. When he rose to speak, I could tell by the look on his face something was wrong—he had a nervous, worn out look, and I didn't know what was going to happen next. Choking back tears, he shared that his daughter, Melissa, had been raped, and she conceived a child. Through his tears, he shared his family couldn't get through such a difficult time without the help of the church.

And that was it. The beginning of my journey. Melissa decided to keep her baby, and her family appeared to circle around her to protect her, as well as their soon-to-be grandchild, and nephew. Our church also stepped up to provide spiritual support, and to help meet the immediate needs for the upcoming changes in their home. The women of the church threw a surprise baby shower, and Melissa was thrilled to receive the necessities for her new baby. Doug handcrafted a cradle especially for Melissa, and as I grew to know Doug's family better, I admired Melissa and her family. I finally understood why Melissa was reluctant to attend church—she was experiencing a trial that would change her life forever.

In retrospect, I know God had a master plan for my life—little did I know how my relationship with Doug, Melissa, and their family would change when the phone call came for Doug to head to the hospital.

That baby changed my life, and he touched so many lives over the next twenty years.

5

The News Spreads

The day before Thanksgiving was an emotional blur—our son was dead, and the news spread like wildfire among our friends and family. Before we knew it, we had a house full of visitors, and our kitchen counter was overflowing with casseroles and desserts.

I asked the Casualty Support Officer what to expect from the media, and he informed me there was a twenty-four hour restriction on the release of information regarding Heath's death. Our story would miss the Thanksgiving Day news cycles, but the press would definitely find out on Friday. I asked a close friend to handle media requests, and she agreed to meet us at nine on Friday morning. She also assured me everything would be okay.

Visitors stayed late into the night, and Heath's friends decided to spend the night to take care of

Ashton and Chandler. After the last visitor's goodbyes, Melissa and I were alone with our raw pain and emotions.

We couldn't sleep—the shock sent our bodies into epinephrine overdrive with adrenaline levels that wouldn't allow us to relax. Going to bed would have been futile, so we just sat up in bed. The tears wouldn't stop and when I finally drifted off, I awoke to the sound of Melissa's sobs. My weeping snapped Melissa awake every time she began to doze, and both of us cried in our sleep. Our tears were overwhelming and endless, and we had never known such gut-wrenching pain.

Heath's friends convinced Ashton and Chandler to play video games downstairs, but it wasn't long before Ashton wandered back to us, and eventually surrendered to exhaustion. Laughter drifted up the stairs as the kids played video games, and all I could think about was Heath would never join them again for a late night video-game fest.

Giving up on sleep, Melissa decided to work on the turkey for our Thanksgiving meal. We decided to continue with our Thanksgiving plans despite our tragedy—we needed the support of our family and friends more than ever.

As morning dawned, we numbly prepared the table. Though Chandler and Ashton watched the Macy's Day parade, the day was nothing like Thanksgivings when music and laughter filled the house. The boys usually clamored for a taste of the Thanksgiving meal, so we always shared dinner rolls mid-morning before guests arrived. Now, the house was eerily silent, and we moved as if we were robots. We didn't have our special rolls in the morning, and the haunting sounds of weeping replaced the music. The phone's ringing shattered our silence around ten, and it was my mom.

"Scott, I just want to warn you—Channel Five from Cleveland is on its way to your house."

I was livid! How did this happen? Mom explained one of my uncles contacted the news station, unthinking in his despair.

"Call them back, Mom," I pleaded. "Tell them to turn around—I don't want reporters intruding today, so please ask them to give us some peace. It's Thanksgiving!" I quickly learned, however, it isn't how the media works. They were coming, whether I invited them or not. In a panic, I called my friend.

"Scott, you need to develop a public statement," she advised. "It just needs to be a few sentences."

I can do this. I stared at the pen in my hand, mentally willing the words to come, but images of Heath filled my mind. The small boy proudly showing off the first fish he ever caught. The ninth grader earnestly expressing his desire to protect freedom by becoming a Marine. The teenager playfully urging me to take him on a late-night fast-food run. The young man behind the wheel for the first time, nervously obeying my directives from the passenger seat. The rookie Marine waving goodbye to his family from the airline security gate. How could I capture Heath in a few sentences for a television reporter?

I couldn't.

I called her back, and I begged. "Please come over to help with the media—we can't do it ourselves."

Even though my friend had visiting family in town, she gave up time with them to come over to help us prepare a statement for the press. She recognized our inability to deal with the press, and her help was invaluable. The final draft read:

As we celebrate Thanksgiving, we give thanks for the privilege of being American, and we pray for our son, and all of the men and women who serve our country so bravely. We love our son and are proud of him, and we honor his sacrifice so we can be free.

We also asked for prayers, and we requested the community of northeast Ohio fly their American flags in honor of Heath.

Within minutes, WEWS Channel 5 News on Your Side arrived at our house, and my friend met the crew on the front porch, sharing our prepared statement. The reporter requested a picture of Heath, and Melissa handed her the formal Marine boot camp photo of him that we displayed in our front room. In his dress blues, he looked solemn and intense— the perfect Marine.

We knew as soon as one news source found out about Heath's death, it would spread to all the news agencies. Soon, it wouldn't be only Channel 5 knocking on our door, but also every newspaper, television, and radio station in the Cleveland metro area.

My sister, Valerie, came over to help us because she was the ideal person to handle the media. Her keen negotiating skills enabled her to handle news organizations with ease, and my publicist friend was kind enough to give Valerie a quick lesson about how to handle the press. Valerie was determined to protect us while providing reporters with enough information to satisfy their requests.

When the doorbell rang, Valerie opened the door to an onslaught of questions. She shared the prepared statement, and let photographers snap a picture of Heath's photo. She collected business cards, as well as letting the reporters know we planned to conduct interviews in the future. Several stations took video footage of our home, our neighborhood and, even though it was Thanksgiving Day, some reporters went to McKinley Senior High

School to see if anyone who knew Heath would share comments. Another reporter interviewed local residents enjoying a fun game of touch football. They were among the first community members to hear about Heath's death, and they were stunned the war had hit so close to home. The doorbell continued to ring throughout the day, but my sister gracefully managed to shield us from media curiosity.

I set the formal dinner table, as well as an additional table, and that's where Melissa, Chandler, Ashton, and I sat. Melissa's parents, my parents and sister, and two of our neighbors sat at the formal table. I wanted—I needed—to be close to our family and, despite our grief coupled with the distractions of the media, we attempted to enjoy a traditional Thanksgiving meal.

However, Heath's empty seat was more than we could bear. Everything began to blur as grief began to overwhelm me, and I can't remember if we said a prayer—all I thought about was Heath's last Thanksgiving. During dinner, he gorged himself on turkey and other favorite foods he missed so much during his strict military training. I couldn't comprehend he would never again be with us, physically, on Thanksgiving.

So it was, and our traditional Thanksgiving changed forever. The laughter and joyful voices normally filling the house were absent. We tried to eat, but the sorrow was overwhelming, and Melissa tearfully left the table within five minutes. I followed shortly after, and Melissa lay sobbing on Heath's bed while I cried in our bedroom. My mom silently entered the room and laid her hand on my arm, trying to absorb the pain. After a few moments, she left to help Melissa. We were so distraught that we left Ashton and Chandler alone downstairs, not knowing who was there to help them deal with their grief. Though we hadn't meant for it to happen, we were beginning to learn each person's grief was separate, and we would grieve in our own ways.

News reporters knocked on the front door throughout the day, family and friends came to visit and, by evening, the house was full. We gathered around the television for the five o'clock news, and Heath's death was the lead story. The room filled with cries and gasps when Heath's picture appeared on the screen. .Ashton was inconsolable, and he couldn't handle seeing his brother's face on television. We turned it off, and decided we wouldn't watch the news anymore. Shock came in waves, and as we grieved the loss of our son, we had to negotiate with the media, as well.

On Thanksgiving night, we awakened crying, and we even cried in our sleep. During a bout of fitful sleep, I had a vision of Heath—I awakened to see Heath in his dress blues standing at the base of my bed, saluting me. It was startling, but comforting.

I fell back to sleep—but, when I awakened again, Heath stood before me still in his dress blues, making special movements with his gloved hands. I later learned the meaning of the vision.

Melissa and I were up by 5:00 A.M., and it was the beginning of a long, very appropriately named, Black Friday. We were in the beginning stages of mourning while the rest of the country was Christmas shopping. We began cleaning the house and, after cleaning up from Thanksgiving, I headed to Kinko's to make copies of the casualty report. I whited out Heath's personal details and, based on the reporters' requests from the previous day, I composed a fact sheet so I wouldn't have to repeat basic information. I also made a sign for the fence at the front of the house to honor Heath. The sign displayed Heath's formal Marine portrait with the inscription, *Honoring Our Hero, January 2, 1987 – November 22, 2006.* While at Kinko's, I received a call from Melissa—reporters were lining up in front of the house.

With copies in hand, I headed home, faced reporters, and distributed the fact sheets—but the reporters wanted interviews, so Melissa and I decided to grant their wishes. We knew if we didn't tell Heath's story others would, and Melissa and I completely believed in our son, as well as his mission. We were sad and proud of him, and we wanted to share our story of this remarkable young man who died in Iraq for the right reasons. It was important to convey Heath's life with honor and dignity—and that he died fighting for his beliefs.

I shared his dream of being a Marine, and his going to Iraq. I shared his love for God, family and country, and his wanting to protect us. He was a bright, intelligent young man who could have chosen safer paths to forge his future, but it was God's calling to be a Marine.

Lori Monsewicz, a reporter from the *Canton Repository,* provided one of the earliest stories, and she captured our early feelings very well in her November 25, 2006, article:

McKinley High School graduate Heath D. Warner had dreamed of becoming a U.S. Marine. When the 19-year-old was "killed instantly by the blast" from an IED (improvised explosive device) during hostilities in Haqlaniya, Iraq, on Wednesday morning, he died just that—a Marine, Private First Class.

"We need men and women like Heath to serve our country, so we can have the privileges we have. I'm in awe of my son," Scott Warner said Friday, fighting back tears as he spoke to media in his living room ...

[Heath] loved to spend time with his family, [his mother] said, calling him "very nurturing" and

pointing out that his younger brothers—Chandler, 14, and Ashton, 7,—"just adored him." She said Chandler was Heath Warner's best friend, and said that when he was home last, Ashton "was on him like Velcro."

[Melissa Warner called] their son, "a wonderful, wonderful young man. He was a hero, and his heart was in it 100 percent," she said.

As we moved through the day, the house buzzed with phone calls, visitors, florists, and reporters. We wore down quickly and, around 2:00 P.M., two local Gold Star families called on us. The Seesans and Rameys lost their sons in the Iraq war, too, and they understood our pain and confusion. We were so grateful for their emotional and practical support— they prepared us regarding what to expect in the days ahead, and it was a blessing to meet these new friends. Until then, we didn't know the Gold Star is a designation by the Department of Defense that honors families whose loved ones are lost in combat.

One of our immediate questions was how to select a mortuary with experience in military funerals, and the Seesans suggested their friends, Jeff and Cathi Heitger, owners of Heitger Funeral Services. Not only were the Heitgers a military family with a son in the Marine Reserves, they also provided the funeral services for the Seesan's son, Aaron.

"You will never have closure unless you have Jeff Heitger determine whether Heath's body is viewable," Tom said. "At the very least, ask if you can see Heath, so you can identify him."

Their advice left us stunned.

We hadn't even thought that far ahead! The Seesan's were devastated when the military notified them their son wasn't viewable. However, with their permission, Jeff Heitger unwrapped Aaron's body and determined they could see, and identify, their son. Jeff's compassionate action gave them a sense of closure, and they were incredibly grateful.

The Rameys, however, weren't permitted to view their son, Richard, and it haunts them to this day.

"We needed to see Richard one last time, but we never got the chance," his mom told me.

There are a couple of sayings in the Gold Star Family community—*it's the one club you don't want to be part of*, and, *I wouldn't wish it on my worst enemy*. However, only the members of this unique club understand each other, and are able to help each other. I'm grateful to the Seesans and Rameys for coming to the house, and leading us through the early stages of the grieving process.

Thankfully, the day started to slow down, and guests and reporters slowly dissipated. We didn't feel like cooking, so Melissa and I made plans to go out for dinner. November 24th was our sixteenth wedding anniversary, and we wanted some private time together. Arriving at the restaurant where we traditionally celebrate our anniversary, we sat in a private booth in the far corner of the room. As we ate, we were aware of how good it felt to be away from home, even if it were only for a brief time. We craved peace and quiet without the drama of our son's death overwhelming us, and we treasured each other's company.

We were recognized, though, and the stares from diners clued us in they knew we were the parents of fallen hero, Pvt. Heath Warner. After we finished our dinner, our server arrived, carrying two desserts—she told us the restaurant managers wanted to do something special—the desserts were called *A Little Bit of Heaven on Earth*. Such a simple gesture and pure act of kindness meant the world to us, and we wished our little bit of Heaven, Heath, was with us again.

"If we are going to survive this, we can't go through another day like today," I told Melissa.

She agreed. Many people offered to help, and I called a friend to ask if she could arrange to have someone at the house each day until the funeral events concluded. They were our angels because we couldn't have survived the coming weeks without them—they greeted guests, answered the phone, received gifts, prepared food, and protected us. They made certain we ate, even though we would forget to eat. When we fell asleep during the day, they watched our home for us. They walked the early steps of grieving with us, and helped us survive.

There was no mistaking it—our family was shattered by war.

6

Love Finds a Way

Melissa was visiting with her brother while I played blocks on the floor with Heath. Heath was a cute little guy, and I enjoyed it when he and Melissa came to visit. By age two, he could already operate the VHS by himself, and he loved to watch Disney Sing-Along videos, and *Land before Time.* His sweet spirit caused him to cry each time Little Foot's mother died in the movie—and I knew it was a sure sign Heath loved his mother.

Over time, my friendship with Melissa grew— we talked and laughed, and it seemed as if we connected. I was focused on trying to get a career started, and Melissa was a single mother doing the best she could to raise Heath. She was fortunate her parents were so supportive—in many ways, her parents were not only grandparents, but also parental figures in young Heath's life. Similarly, Doug was more than an uncle to Heath. Melissa's family reminded me of my own because they were

Christian, and they held many of the same values as my family. Melissa's father was an electrician, her mother a homemaker, and they provided a strong foundation for Melissa during Heath's early years.

On Valentine's Day, 1989, Melissa dropped off dinner for Doug at the apartment, and, to my surprise, she gave me a Valentine's Day card, too. It was a Care Bear card, and I interpreted its message in two ways: *from a friend to a friend*, or, *I like you*. The card haunted me in a good way for weeks and, as Melissa and I spent more time together, she was no longer Doug's little sister. She was a very attractive woman with stunning blue eyes, beautiful red hair, and a smile that could light up a room! She was confident, and I was impressed with how she handled being a single mother, as well as how completely devoted she was to Heath.

As our friendship developed, I was smitten by her beautiful blue eyes and smile, and I had a secret crush. But I wasn't sure if the card were just a friendship card. *Does she feel the same way I do? Does she like me for more than a friend, or just as a friend?* I wrestled with these questions for some time, and I sought advice from several friends. I wanted to ask Melissa out, but there was a lot at stake—Melissa had a child, and I couldn't take that lightly. *Am I mature enough to be an instant father?* I knew I couldn't enter this dating relationship casually, because Melissa and Heath could be hurt. I wasn't certain where to turn, so I turned to God—and I prayed about pursuing a dating relationship. I was twenty-five at the time, and after some reflection and talking with close friends, I decided to ask her to go to lunch with me. It seemed like a logical first step toward taking our friendship to the next level, and I also felt if I approached the relationship slowly, it might help determine how things could work out between Heath and me. I figured if I started dating Melissa, I had to be prepared to be an instant father. I thought and prayed about this decision and, as I began to mature and prepare for the future, I knew I wanted to be married, and a father. It was clear Melissa would be a great mother to our children, and that was imperative to me.

So, one week after church, I finally worked up my courage.

"Will you please ask your parents to watch Heath this afternoon?" I asked Melissa, trying to seem casual even though my heart was pounding. "I'd like to take you to lunch, and then we can run over to the mall."

I didn't even have time to hold my breath—her face immediately lit up with a smile and, luckily, her parents agreed to take Heath home. I was ecstatic! *Of course, this isn't a date*, I told myself. *It's just two friends having lunch.*

We lunched at Friday's, and shopped at the mall—I tried on several pairs of shorts and asked Melissa's opinion, and I laughed to myself as I asked her which pair she liked better. I was hoping she liked my legs! It was so much fun that I asked her out on a real date for the following weekend. She didn't hesitate, and we immediately made plans.

That week, I could think of little else. *What if Melissa only views me as her brother's friend? Will we lose our easy-going friendship under the pressure of a date?* I dated several girls previously, but Melissa was someone special. Everything had to be just right—I bought a new shirt for the occasion, and I paid meticulous attention to my appearance before picking her up on Saturday evening.

My hand shook slightly as I knocked on her door—she answered, wearing a new outfit that exactly matched my new shirt! We dissolved in laughter, and my nerves settled—she was just my friend. Melissa. We were perfect together. Our date consisted of watching the movie *Rain Man*, enjoying dinner at Max and Erma's, and topping off the evening with coffee at Denny's.

Some people know they're with the right person, and that's how I felt about Melissa. I had butterflies in my stomach, and I couldn't stop thinking about her. As my feelings intensified, I finally confessed to some close friends I was falling in love. Actually, I knew from the first date we were going to get married ...

At church, Melissa's family sat up front as usual, but with one change. Instead of sitting on the outside next to Doug, I switched seats with Doug, and sat next to Melissa. The simple switch wasn't unnoticed—everyone knew we were a couple. And, as our dating relationship became serious, I told Melissa how much I loved her ... but ... I warned her my life was like a roller coaster ride, and if she couldn't handle it, she should get off. Not certain how to interpret my comment, Melissa asked me what I meant.

"I'm not your typical person," I told her. "I like doing things on the edge, and if you can't handle that, then I'm probably not the right person for you."

As I waited for her answer, I thought of the challenges ahead. I was leaving for graduate school in Virginia Beach in the fall, while Melissa would stay in Ohio with her son, at least for a while. Heath was comfortable living with his mom and grandparents, but if my relationship with Melissa had a future, Heath would have to accept me as a part of his life, too.

"I want to ride the roller coaster of life with you, Scott," she answered. "I'm in love with you, too."

Leaving Melissa was agonizing because we were still reveling in our new relationship, each day discovering something new and delightful about each other. Moving to another state when we were getting serious seemed wrong, but I was committed to attending graduate school at Regent University's Master of Arts in Government program, and specializing in Public Policy. Politics were a part of my life since I was young, and President Ronald Reagan deeply inspired me. He wore his patriotism on his sleeve, and ended the cold war without firing a single shot—I knew I couldn't give up the chance.

That summer, Melissa's worst fear was I would break off the relationship after I arrived at Regent. Before I left for Virginia in August, 1989, I prepared a gift basket for her, and I asked her mother to put it next to Melissa's bed. It contained love notes and encouraging Scripture, because I wanted Melissa to know I intended to stay for the long term. There were many, however, who told me I was in a relationship over my head.

"A single mother with a bi-racial son? What are you thinking?" they asked. "Why would a single man with an open field to his future choose this marriage?"

It was a good question, and I looked to the Holy Family of Jesus, Mary and Joseph as my guides to my life's decision. Although an angel didn't appear to Melissa, telling her she would conceive a son and name him Heath, she did find herself in an unplanned crisis pregnancy, as did Mary. And, similar to Mary, she had to make a choice: would she trust God, and say yes to this pregnancy, or would she say no, and abort her child? Melissa's parents raised her in a Christian home, and she strongly believed abortion was murder. Even though she was tempted to abort the baby, she said yes to God, and yes to life.

I found myself in a similar situation as Joseph— I had a choice. If I pursued the relationship and married Melissa, I would become the adoptive father to her little boy. Like Joseph, God did speak to me, as well. I remember when Melissa was pregnant with Heath, I was at church, and there was a clear sightline from where I was standing to where Melissa was standing. As I looked at her, a voice in my head said, "She is going to be your wife." I remember arguing with God during the service. "I'm not going to marry her. She's going to have a child." Also, I wanted a fast-track business career once I finished college, and having a child didn't really factor into it.

It was my calling to marry Melissa, and to be the father of this little boy.

My little boy.

My Heath.

7

Honoring a Hero

It was ten days before Heath came home from Iraq. The vibrant colors of an Ohio autumn gave way to the dull brown of winter, and trees shed the last of their fall foliage, leaving only barren branches silhouetted against the grey December sky. Chill winds from the northwest hinted at snowstorms to come.

My own spirit felt as bleak as the surrounding landscape as we began to make Heath's funeral arrangements. We struggled with uncertainty—there was a delay in choosing a specific day for the ceremony because we didn't have a release date from the military. The Marines were working with Arlington National Cemetery to determine a date for Heath's burial, so as soon as we were notified the burial was to take place on December 12, 2006, we arranged to receive Heath at Cleveland Hopkins International Airport in Cuyahoga County.

The last time we were at the airport, we welcomed Heath home for a three-week visit before his tour of duty in Iraq. As we eagerly waited outside the gate, Heath came running toward us, enveloping us in a wonderful family hug. In my mind's eye, I carried a similar picture of Heath's arrival home from Iraq—I hadn't envisioned a solemn, and sorrowful journey to meet Heath's casket.

But on Saturday, December 2 (Melissa's fortieth birthday), we prepared to welcome home our fallen hero. Cathi Heitger picked us up by limousine for the trip to the airport, and her presence was calming and compassionate. With her own son in the Marine Reserves, she could easily imagine herself in our place, and she truly shared this journey of pain with us. She took painstaking care with every part of Heath's funeral in Canton, hoping it were as dignified as possible.

"Are Chandler and Ashton coming?"

"This is too much for them, Cathi. They're staying with Melissa's parents while we're gone." Melissa and I didn't want the boys to experience such grief.

Darkness fell as we traveled the sixty miles north to meet our son. Green and red Christmas decorations twinkled in the suburbs along I-71, their merriment at odds with our somber moods—we gave up on small talk as we contemplated the task ahead. Cathi advised us against expectations for a hero's welcome for our son—his casket was in a crate, and we were to meet him in the cargo area. That didn't matter to us. We loved Heath, and we didn't want his casket to travel alone from a cold and impersonal warehouse to the funeral home. We wanted to be the first to welcome Heath back to American soil, and we wanted to accompany him home to Stark County.

Though the heat in the car was on full blast, I shivered. Filled with dread, questions raced through my mind. *What will it be like to see his casket for the first time? Will his casket be covered with an American flag? Will the warehouse provide any dignity for our son?* I secretly wondered whether Melissa and I could emotionally survive what we were about to do.

Night cloaked the airport, and when we arrived at the main gate, we weren't allowed to enter.

"I'm going to check to see what's going on," Cathi volunteered, as she hopped from the limousine to talk to airport authorities. While we waited in the car, we were puzzled by what seemed to be an unusual amount of hustle and bustle. It was difficult to see, but several authoritative-looking people gathered around Cathi, talking and gesturing rapidly—in the background, we could see the hearse and van transporting the Marine Honor Guard.

After about fifteen minutes, Cathi opened the car door. "Hey, guys—this is going to be different than I anticipated. There are reporters here wanting to know if you will interview with them—we're going to receive Heath on the tarmac when his plane lands."

Shocked, I envisioned a public spectacle, and I had to put a stop to it. "Cathi, we aren't interested in talking with the reporters," I told her. "This is our oldest son, and we want to greet him honorably, and with dignity."

Cathi promised to take care of it, but Melissa and I realized Heath's homecoming wouldn't be private, after all. We were disconcerted the quiet welcome we expected was suddenly a public event, and neither of us knew how we were going to respond to the situation.

All we wanted was to be alone with our son, and our grief.

The airport closed the surrounding airspace as the commercial airliner carrying Heath's casket circled in over Lake Erie. Police officers, fire trucks, city dignitaries and the Marines escorted Melissa and me onto the tarmac to wait. In the distance, the lights of a single jet approached the runway—my heart raced, and Melissa's hand trembled in mine.

"I'm frightened, Scott," she whispered. I squeezed her hand a little tighter to let her know I understood, and to silently encourage her to be strong.

Cold wind whipped around us as the airliner landed and taxied to where we stood, and passengers remained on the plane until Heath's casket was removed. On the airliner and in the terminal, there were announcements of a fallen hero returning home. Faces pressed against windows as people sought to catch sight of our son. *Oh, God, I can't do this*, I thought as we waited. And then I saw Heath's flag-draped casket. The Marine Honor Guard lingered over his coffin, making certain each detail was perfect, as they carefully adjusted the U.S. flag. Then they gently lowered the casket to a conveyer belt. Six Marines in immaculate dress blues raised their white-gloved hands in a somber salute to their fallen brother, then solemnly escorted the casket to Melissa and me, and placed it in the awaiting hearse. The honor and dignity were palpable, and I thought of pictures of President Kennedy's casket received from Air Force 1—the Marines provided the same level of honor to our son. Time stood still in the bitter wind as we watched Heath receive overwhelming admiration, and esteem for his sacrifice to his country.

The crowd maintained a respectful silence as we touched our son's casket—I'll always remember Melissa's black-velvet-gloved hands carefully pulling back the flag so she could kiss Heath's coffin. The United States flag was never more beautiful, or more meaningful to me than when I saw it draped over Heath's casket on that cold December evening. I knew then freedom isn't free, and the cost of freedom for us was the blood, sweat, and tears of our son.

Reporters with video cameras lined the exit to get shots of the hearse and our limousine as we left the airport. The police escorted us to the Cuyahoga County line, where the Patriot Guard Riders took over. The Patriot Guard is a group of motorcycle riders who honor the military's fallen by showing respect to their families and communities. In addition, they shield the mourning family, and their friends from interruptions created by protestors, and they traveled with us all the way to the funeral home.

"I was so scared," Melissa's whisper broke our silence.

"I know, Honey—I was, too." I held her hand, and we sat close to each other the rest of the drive back to Canton. We were trying to absorb and process what we just witnessed.

At the funeral home, the Marine Honor Guard escorted Heath's casket into the parlor, where they would keep him during his time in Canton. The accompanying officers asked Melissa and me to wait in a lounge outside the parlor while they made sure Heath's uniform was properly dressed with his medals and awards. The lounge was small—almost like a kitchenette—and we sat at the little round table while Cathi poured steaming cups of coffee. Cathi's husband, Jeff, soon joined us.

The Heitger family's mortuary was established in 1869, and it was immediately clear Jeff is dedicated to his profession. His presence was comforting as we talked about Heath, his death and the funeral events that would take place over the next week. Having walked this journey with the Seesans, and having a son in the Marine Reserves, Jeff wasn't doing business as usual—he was emotionally vested in our family, and he and his wife stayed with us until the Marines let us know we could go into the parlor, and spend private time with our son.

The large parlor was set up with rows of chairs, ready to receive hundreds of guests. I felt small in this immense space with just Cathi, Jeff and Melissa beside me. My vision blurred when I saw the casket at the front of the room, knowing Heath was inside it. It was surreal. *Why, God? Why our family? Why our son? Oh, Jesus, please help me get through this!* Life seemed so unfair, and my family couldn't absorb the shock of losing Heath. Yet, there he lay, the American flag covering his closed casket. During the ten days we awaited Heath's return, we avoided the reality of his death. Now, standing before his casket, we knew the painful tasks of his funeral would move us forward. Cathi and Jeff pulled up chairs so we could sit close to Heath, and Melissa's weeping was all we could hear in the room. Melissa didn't stay long, and I was left alone with Heath—through my tears, I asked God to help me change my ways. Prior to November 22, 2006, my priorities in life were skewed. I centered my life on my career, and I put my relationship with God and my family further down on my priority list. I vowed to be a better person, knowing how brave and courageous our son was in life. After about an hour we returned home, mentally and emotionally drained, but glad to be with our friends and family.

Melissa and I wondered if Heath's body would be viewable—I assumed he would be. I thought his vehicle flipped when it encountered the IED, and I imagined Heath catapulting from the vehicle, suffering a broken neck. So, when we were finalizing Heath's funeral arrangements with our Casualty Officer and Cathi Heitger, I asked, "Will Heath be dressed in his own uniform dress blues, or will the Marines be providing another set for him to wear?"

The officer's lip quivered as he replied, "Sir …
Ma'am … Sir, your son will have his dress uniform
laying on top of him." As the full impact of the
Casualty Officer's words hit us, we burst into tears.
Our son's death had been horrific.

Since an IED explosion killed Heath, his body
was severely damaged. We signed a form regarding
how we wanted any additional remains found in the
desert to be handled—did we want to have them
returned to us, or should the military dispose of them
in a dignified manner? It reminded me of a magazine
article I read a few weeks before Heath's death about
the families of victims of the September 11th
terrorist attacks on the World Trade Center. Many
families received multiple remains, having to bury
their loved ones repeatedly. I knew our family
couldn't do that, and we signed the form to have the
military dispose of any additional remains in a
dignified manner. Then the Marine Casualty Officer
handed us our Gold Star pins, and a Gold Star flag to
replace Heath's Blue Star flag in our front window. I
didn't want that pin, and I refused to take down his
Blue Star flag for some time.

Although the military said Heath wasn't
viewable, we wanted some form of physical
identification. Without it, how would we know for
sure if it were Heath in the casket? We asked Cathi

to unwrap Heath's body to determine whether there a way for us to see him.

On Monday, December 4, my cell phone rang, and my hands shook when I saw Cathi's name on the caller ID. I could barely choke out a greeting.

"Well, Scott—Jeff unwrapped Heath's body, and the physical damage is extreme enough that Heath's body is not viewable. I'm so sorry to have to tell you that."

I just closed my eyes, and took a deep breath.

"Scott, are you okay?" Cathi gently asked.

"I'm trying to take this in. Is there any chance we can see any part of him? What about his right arm? Can it be viewed?" Heath had a distinctive Japanese Kanji tattoo on his upper right arm. "If we can just see that tattoo, we will know for sure it's Heath."

Cathi said she would check with Jeff and call back. I kept thinking, *we're too young to have to be going through this.* But we had to know if it were Heath in that casket.

The phone rang again—Cathi told me the most severe damage from the blast's impact was on Heath's left side, and the tattoo was still visible on Heath's right arm. So, Jeff prepared Heath for viewing the next day, and little did we know his act of kindness would later become vital for two bereaved parents.

Melissa and I were tormented as we arrived at the funeral home for our private viewing on December 5th.

"Scott, I don't think I can do this," Melissa said through tears. "Let me go in first," I reassured her. "If I think it's too much, then I'll let you know." Our plan seemed to help Melissa, but both of us were scared.

Cathi greeted us at the door, gave us each a hug, and guided us into the lounge while we waited for Jeff. The few minutes we waited only intensified my anxiety, but I needed to do this as much as I wanted to run from it.

Jeff took me in first.

The flag lay across a few chairs in the funeral parlor, the casket lid was open, and Heath's body was wrapped in a green wool blanket secured by safety pins. Heath's dress blues uniform lay atop the blanket, and all of his medals were in place. I could only think of how handsome Heath had been in is dress blues, and how he beamed with pride. *I can't believe my poor son is so physically damaged that his uniform has to lie on top of him*, I thought.

Jeff was very kind, gentle and patient, and after a few minutes, he lifted the right sleeve. On Heath's bare arm, I saw the familiar Japanese Kanji tattoo. I remembered when he first got it—he hid it from me because he didn't want me to lecture him for desecrating his body. When I saw it, he told me it meant Truth, and I thought that seemed reasonable. Now, as I looked at his arm, I could finally say yes, it was really Heath. The questions I repeatedly asked the Marine Casualty Officers, "Are you sure it's Heath? How do you know it's him?" were finally answered. Our little boy who had innocently played with a tree twig as a gun in the backyard was now a war hero—pride, and sorrow, filled my heart as I looked at his arm.

Now it was Melissa's turn.

This time, Cathi and Jeff walked with Melissa and me into the parlor. Tears cascaded down Melissa's cheeks, and Cathi and I had to hold her up as we approached the casket.

"I'm so sorry you have to go through this, but you need to do this for closure," Cathi spoke quietly. "You need to see it's Heath."

When Jeff lifted Heath's sleeve, Melissa saw the tattoo, and she knew there was no doubt. We all wept, and as we stood there, Jeff and Cathi asked us what the tattoo meant. I was quick to respond that it meant truth, and Melissa began to chuckle.

"Well, actually, it means 'To Kill Evil Instantly', she said. She explained Heath didn't want to hear my lecture on tattoos, so he told me something I would find more acceptable. Jeff, Cathi,

Melissa, and I had a good laugh, and it broke the tension of the moment.

They told us it was okay to touch him, and we began to touch our child's body for the last time. I felt his cold arm. My hands traced his face, head, chest, and legs—he definitely bulked up while he was overseas. When I thought of Heath in Iraq, I imagined his working his fingers to the bone—calloused hands with dirt under his nails. When I saw him in the casket, I looked at his right hand—it was calloused with dirt under his nails. His life in the desert must have been as hard as I had imagined.

As I stood before Heath, memories of our family flooded my brain—our everyday lives together—vacations, school memories, the laughter with his friends and brothers, his break dancing, and his fierce devotion to the military. And now, overwhelming sorrow.

Once we closed the lid to his casket, I knew it would be the end of our family, as we knew it.

And, it was.

8

A Public Service, and Our Private Grief

How do you plan a funeral for a fallen hero? There isn't a how-to book, and a military funeral follows its own protocol. We found ourselves in the center of an unfamiliar military world, and at the center of media attention. But, with the grace of God, family and friends, we somehow navigated the process. Unable to sleep, I wandered into my office to check emails and respond to condolences. As I sat there, visions of an honorable funeral filled my head, and I believed an inspirational patriotic service would most honor Heath, God, his family, friends, and our great country. I sketched the front of the church sanctuary with pictures of Heath on display on the big screens, his casket centered between, and his favorite music filling the room. I had one more idea for honoring

Heath, but I wasn't sure the funeral home would agree. So I shared my idea with Melissa, and we agreed that Heath should receive all the honor of a hero, but we wanted to do it with dignity. I invited Cathi to our home to discuss Heath's funeral plans, and to make my request in person.

"Okay—I know this is different, and kind of out there—but Melissa and I want an antique, horse-drawn hearse to carry Heath through Canton." My heart was set on doing something truly special for my son, and I pictured a slow, stately journey through the city, allowing members of the community to say goodbye to one of their own. I watched Cathi carefully, certain she would say no.

"Okay, let me see what I can do," she answered, taking a deep breath. After discussing plans for the funeral in Canton, and Heath's burial at Arlington National Cemetery, Cathi left to begin making arrangements. So I was surprised when she called a short time later, asking to come over to the house again. I assumed she needed to go over a few more details for Heath's funeral.

When she arrived, I knew her visit was about more than funeral details—her face was pale and drawn, her usual compassionate expression replaced with one of concern. She asked us to sit down at the table, and we waited expectantly while she struggled for words.

"I have to share some information that's going to upset you," she said.

I thought, *what could possibly be worse than the death of our son?*

"I was notified that Westboro Church is filing for permits with the City of Canton to protest at Heath's funeral."

Melissa and I were stunned! I was vaguely familiar with the church—I heard they disrupted the funerals of fallen heroes to make a statement against war. Suddenly, all I could see was a horde of shouting, angry protestors carrying anti-war placards, spoiling the peace and dignity of my oldest son's funeral. Westboro Church's sentiments are incomprehensible—they carry signs reading, *God Hates the USA*, *Thank God for IEDs*, and *Thank God for Dead Soldiers.* I was already planning to leap from the limousine to confront them if they appeared during Heath's funeral procession. He gave his life for his country, and I wasn't about to let such people defile his name.

"I know this is the last thing you want to hear," Cathi continued, "but the Patriot Guard Riders offered to serve as a barrier between the protestors, and your family." We definitely wanted the protection of the Patriot Guard, and Cathi continued to explain the Westboro Church often filed for permits, and then they wouldn't show up. We prayed they would stay away from Heath's funeral.

Visitation hours were from three to nine on Tuesday, December 5, 2006, and I recall getting dressed for my son's viewing was the strangest feeling. In our little family, suits and ties were usually reserved for weddings, festive and happy occasions. Now, we were dressing in our best for just the opposite—a sad, unwanted event. I straightened Chandler and Ashton's ties, Melissa inspected them, gave them a hug and a kiss, and we reluctantly climbed into the car.

The ride to the church was silent. Family members greeted us at the church, and others were there as well, eager to provide emotional support.

"I want to take you in so you can have some private time with Heath before more guests arrive," Cathi said as she led us past the visitors.

Each of us took a deep breath.

An American flag spanned the entire front wall, serving as a backdrop for Heath's flag-draped casket. A Marine in dress blues stood at attention at the head of his casket, and at Heath's feet lay a beautiful white rose wreath, carefully selected by Melissa and me, and designed by a friend of ours who is a florist. Floral arrangements spilled into the aisle as a testimony to the many lives he had touched.

We all clung to each other and sat down in the front pew, trying to absorb the scene. The church was awkwardly silent, and after a few moments, Cathi left us alone with Heath. Melissa and I approached his casket, placing our hands on it, and leaning over to give Heath a kiss. I turned to look at Ashton and Chandler, and my heart ached at the sight of their blank, anxious stares. This was their first view of their brother's casket. I asked if I could walk them up to the casket, but they both said no. They were frightened enough just to be in the sanctuary for their brother's viewing—placing their hands on his coffin was more than they could handle.

Melissa and I were numb as we sat and stared at the casket, periodically touching it as if to let Heath know we were there. Our gazes inched down the casket, looking at family photos—our last vacation at Disney World was the last family portrait with Heath. His senior picture. We also read the cards from friends and family accompanying the flower arrangements. I felt disconnected from reality, and I wondered how this could this really being happening to us.

I dreaded the next few hours.

"A lot of people will be coming through the church tonight," I whispered to Melissa. "We have to extend grace to people who say stupid things to us." I was grateful to everyone who came to the calling hours to remember Heath and support our family, but their well-meaning comments often cut deeply. Melissa was already thinking the same thing.

During the weeks preceding the funeral, we were told, "You should be happy Heath is in Heaven," or, "God must have really needed him, and that is why He took him," or, "Well, you still have your other children." I had to bite my lip to keep from shouting in reply, "Yes, we have other children, but I want Heath back!" Even so, we were determined no matter how deep our personal grief and pain, we would handle the calling hours with dignity.

After about twenty minutes, Cathi asked if we were ready to start receiving guests. A line was already forming, and Melissa and I stood with our parents to greet the visitors who were coming to extend their sympathies. Ashton and Chandler left to find their cousins and friends.

A slideshow of Heath's life played on television screens at the front of the church—Heath as a toddler, jumping out of a beautifully wrapped Christmas package with a mischievous grin, ten-year-old Heath and four-year-old Chandler, asleep on Heath's bed with sheets wrapped around their heads, their faces visible, as if they fell asleep looking into each other's eyes. Ashton lying across

Heath's lap at the bottom of the stairs, playing Nintendo games. Heath's Marine boot camp graduation—it was such a celebration, and we were so proud Heath achieved his dream.

As memories of Heath's life flashed on the screen, the words of his favorite song, *Free Bird*, by Lynyrd Skynyrd echoed through the room:

If I leave here tomorrow,
Would you still remember me?
For I must be traveling on now,
'Cause there's too many places I've got to see

The lyrics of *Arlington* by Trace Adkins haunted me, as I recalled taking Heath to Arlington National Cemetery when he was about ten years old. He stood at the tomb of the Unknown Soldier, his small arm raised in a salute to the Army Honor Guard, a look of wonder and longing on his face. Now, Arlington would be his final resting place.

And every time I hear twenty-one guns,
I know they brought another hero home to us
We're thankful for those thankful for the things we've
done,
We can rest in peace, 'cause we are the chosen ones,
We made it to Arlington, yea dust to dust,
Don't cry for us, we made it to Arlington.

A Public Service, and our Private Grief

In *American Soldier* by Toby Keith, I could almost hear Heath speaking the lyrics to me. Before he left for Iraq, he told me he wanted to fight over there so we wouldn't have to fight them over here. He counted the cost, and he was willing to pay the ultimate price.

And I will always do my duty no matter what the
price.
I've counted up the cost, I know the sacrifice
Oh, and I don't want to die for you
But if dyin's asked of me.
I'll bear that cross with honor
'Cause freedom don't come free

Several thousand people came to the viewing, and between the songs, the slideshow, and photo collages of Heath's childhood, each guest took a journey through Heath's life with us. We later learned that many visitors turned away because it was taking two to three hours to reach our family. One man with two preschool-age boys waited patiently through the long line to greet us.

"Mr. Warner, I'm so sorry for your loss, and sacrifice of your son," the father said, shaking my hand.

"Thank you for coming," I replied as I reached down to shake the hands of his two little boys. "I noticed your standing in line with your sons, and I have to compliment you on how well behaved they were while waiting such a long time."

"Well, Mr. Warner, I want my sons to meet the parents of an American Hero." The boys handed me an American flag, and it brought me to tears. I'll never forget this family's simple gesture, or the patience of the young boys who wanted to learn all about an American hero.

The outpouring of love and respect from the community was overwhelming, and at nine thirty in the evening Cathi approached us, suggesting we end the viewing. We left the line, and the remainder of the guests walked by Heath's casket to pay their final respects. After we returned home, we were in awe of what we experienced that evening— it wasn't a sad night—instead, we felt supported, honored, and inspired.

We kept saying to each other, "Heath wouldn't believe it." He was a simple, kindhearted person, and not one to draw attention to himself … and that made the events of the night more special. I could see Heath looking down from Heaven with a big smile on his face. Before we went to bed that night, I put the final touches on the eulogy for Heath's funeral service the next day.

A Public Service, and our Private Grief

December 6, 2006, dawned cold and grey, and snow spit in the frigid air. I didn't know what to expect at Heath's funeral, but I prayed God would lead our family through the day ahead. We arrived at the church at eleven o'clock for a private service for the family. And although the church was where we attended weekly services, it seemed alien to us that day. We were saying goodbye to our son, and our time with him on earth in a physical sense was nearing its end. I wanted to freeze everything, so we didn't have to move closer to our final goodbye—but I couldn't. I had to see it through.

Many members of our family had already arrived, and we greeted each other with hugs and kisses. The good news of the moment was the Westboro Church wasn't present—they sought permits to gain media attention with no intention of showing up. It was an answer to prayer, and we proceeded in peace.

It was important for our immediate family members to have time with Heath, and us, before the public service at one o'clock. In appreciation for their love and support of our son, we gave each member of the family a special Christmas ornament with Heath's picture.

Guests began to arrive and, as promised, the Patriot Guard lined the walk in front of the church, holding American flags. I took Ashton out to meet

them in their black leather vests, coats, and Harley
Davidson gear. We shook hands, and thanked each
of them for coming and supporting our family.

Whether from the cold or from nerves, I was
shaking as the funeral began. The church was packed
to capacity, and the service began with a prelude and
patriotic video to the music of *Battle Hymn of the
Republic*. We entered the church to the mournful
sound of bagpipes playing the Marine Corps Hymn,
and family and friends squeezed together in every
pew to make room for the hundreds of guests
wanting to honor Heath's memory. We took our
seats, and a beautiful service began to unfold. Our
cousin led the congregation in the Pledge of
Allegiance, followed by our dear friend who sang
America the Beautiful. As the familiar words flowed
over the guests, I felt God's presence—everyone in
the congregation sang *God Bless America* with pride
for Heath, our family and country.

Heath's best friends and his uncle Doug shared
their memories of Heath—his friends were also part
of his breakdancing crew. And, as Melissa's birthing
coach, Doug helped Heath enter the world, and it
seemed fitting that Doug lead us in saying goodbye.

I presented the main eulogy, because Melissa
and I decided no one else knew Heath better. I began
with a formal, public expression of condolences to

the families of the service members killed with Heath in the explosion.

I then quoted from a collection of drawings from Ashton's classmates entitled *Your Brother was a Hero*.

"A Hero is strong."

"A Hero helps other people."

"A Hero is brave."

"A Hero is special."

"Though simple in thought, these phrases described Heath—our hero."

My eulogy addressed Heath's love for God, family, and country:

Heath loved his family. All of us. Heath was a selfless, simple person. He loved his mother, father, and brothers, Chandler and Ashton. We were a happy family of five. Chandler and Heath developed a special friendship, and had many goofy late movie nights together, and Ashton was his 'brothee'—it was his nickname for Heath. He could count on Heath for that special toy and Chinese food.

Heath and I were just transitioning from the parent-child to the parent-friend relationship. My last alone time with Heath was dinner at Carrabba's, and a movie at Tinsel Town before he left.

However, when I think of his love of family, I

have to share about a special love between a mother and a son. At the age of nineteen, a single Melissa found herself in a crisis pregnancy, and in the midst of this trauma, Melissa found strength to give her child life.

Melissa put her entire being into raising Heath. Not long ago, Heath thanked his mother for giving him the gift of life. Heath understood what his mother did for him, and he seized the moment to follow his dreams.

I couldn't help but honor Melissa for her special relationship with Heath. She gave it her all. She gave him the best of the best of what she had to give him. I presented Melissa with a spectacular bouquet of roses, for which she received a standing ovation from the congregation.

I ended my eulogy with our experiences of sending Heath off to war:

As we sent Heath off to war, it was the hardest thing his mother and I ever had to do. Heath knew death was a possible reality, and we struggled with this. However, Heath accepted his mission, and he was willing to finish it to the end. On November 22, 2006, God took our son in His arms, and left a hero in his place.

Today we honor our hero, Pvt. Heath D. Warner, beloved son, brother, grandson, nephew, cousin, and friend. May your blood on foreign land feed, and produce a harvest of freedom. May your selflessness be remembered through all the years, because I know that when you were fighting you were thinking of all of us.

May God bless you, may God bless America, and may God bless the men and women serving for freedom across this world.

The Christian and patriotic music, as well as the memories of friends and family truly gave honor to our son. I stored these treasures in my heart as I began to say goodbye to my child.

Amazing Grace echoed from the bagpipes as we exited the church, and a crowd of people waited outside. Cameras clicked as Melissa and I approached the antique glass hearse to touch Heath's casket. With heads bowed, Melissa, Chandler, Ashton, and I huddled together, arms around each other. We didn't want to say goodbye, but in silent tears we let go.

Our limousine was specially decorated with the Marine Eagle, Globe, and Anchor. It was a rare sight to see a flag-covered casket with a Marine in full dress uniform sitting next to the driver of the horse drawn carriage. The bagpipes continued to play *Amazing Grace* as the procession began.

The clip-clop of horse hooves on the pavement created a solemn rhythm that captured the attention of the hundreds of people lining the street, holding banners that read, *Thank you, Heath, We love you, Heath,* and *God Bless America.* We passed the fire station, and firefighters saluted Heath as the procession turned into the Park of the Presidents. The two black horses pulling the flagged-draped coffin with the Marine Honor Guard and driver towering above them made a perfect picture against the barren trees and grey skies.

The procession moved through the park carrying Heath past our home one last time. Neighbors waving American flags lined the sidewalks, and they planted flags along the street. As we neared our house, Christmas wreaths sparkled in windows as a stark reminder this and all future holidays would be something less than they had once been.

The hearse passed Worley Elementary School where Heath attended as a child. Ashton's classmates were outside waving flags, and we lowered the window so Ashton could say hi to his friends, and teacher. The schoolyard fence was a field of yellow ribbons …

On our final pass, we lowered the windows, waved, and thanked the many residents from our community who lined the streets—many said thank you, and God bless you as we passed by.

Once we pulled into the church parking lot, the full Marine Honor Guard was waiting to receive Heath, and to transfer him into the hearse that would take him back to the Heitger Funeral Home. Heath would stay there overnight before being transported back to Cleveland Hopkins International Airport for a flight to Washington, D.C. Until his burial at Arlington National Cemetery the following week, a local funeral home would keep Heath.

Many family members and Heath's friends came back to the house. We also invited the Marine escort who accompanied Heath through this entire process. The events of the day were so inspiring, family and friends stayed until eleven o'clock. By then we were exhausted and ready to gear down for the night.

We escorted Heath to the airport the following morning, but this time was much different. Melissa and I drove separately, and we followed the hearse to the airport. Heath's coffin was crated, and when we arrived, he was taken to the cargo warehouse. We had our final glimpse of Heath's casket during processing for the flight to Washington, D.C., and it was from this point forward we trusted our loved one into the care of the U.S. Army.

9

Where Valor Rests

On Monday, December 11, 2006, we were hastily trying to finish our packing before catching our flight to Washington, D.C.

"Melissa, what are you wearing at Arlington?" I called out uncertainly as I stared into my closet. There would be military, family, friends, and news cameras surrounding us, and I wanted to be certain my appearance honored my son.

"I'm not sure. I think I'm going to wear my black velvet pant suit." Melissa had a flurry of last-minute details on her mind, and I could tell she was distracted.

"Scott, make sure you pack the boys' suits," she called. "And we should pack winter coats just in case it's cold." There was so much to do, but before we knew it our Casualty Officer arrived to pick us up, and he was ringing the doorbell.

Up until now, our contact with Arlington Administration was limited. The Navy Chaplain called with instructions one week before the burial, and I was to provide a list of guests. Heath's hearse would arrive from the funeral home, so we were to meet at the Administration Building prior to the burial and, once our guests were assembled, we were to follow the hearse to Section 60 where the fallen from Iraq and Afghanistan are buried. The chaplain would offer comments and a prayer, and the entire service would last about fifteen minutes. It was our understanding Arlington National Cemetery conducted twenty-five to thirty-five burials daily, and they had to keep a tight schedule.

The chaplain previously asked us about permitting media to be present—we wanted to keep the service dignified, but we also wanted the public to see it. We felt it important the community view the cost of freedom—however, we were against interviews after the burial at Arlington.

We asked Cathi to locate a videographer and photographer to capture Heath's burial service so we could preserve his sacrifice for future generations of Warners. I requested photographs of the family at the Arlington House, as well.

Though the details were coming together, I consulted Melissa because I felt uneasy after my conversation with the chaplain.

"Do you realize there's nothing personal about Heath included in his burial?" I asked. "I don't like this—it feels too impersonal and sterile."

She agreed. We decided someone close to Heath needed to speak at the service, even with the tight schedule.

Our pastor and his wife were traveling with us for the Arlington ceremony, so I called him to request his sharing a few comments at the gravesite. In addition, I wanted to read a poem by Aaron Seesan, who was the son of the Gold Star family we met after learning of Heath's death. Aaron, ultimately sacrificing his own life in war, wrote the poem during his senior year of high school, and I felt his words described Heath—I hoped they would help everyone at the ceremony understand my son.

Before leaving for the airport, we decided to call the Navy chaplain and, after greeting him warmly, I made our request, hoping it wouldn't be too far outside of military protocol.

There was a moment of silence as the chaplain considered the question, and he told me he would have to clear our request with officials at the cemetery. With that, we hung up, and I waited for a return call. After a few seemingly endless minutes, the phone rang.

"Hi, Chaplain, I hope you have good news for us?"

"The administration approved your requests," he answered. "But, we'll need to keep things moving, and your pastor's comments must be brief." I promised to take care of the arrangements on our end.

On the way to the airport, our driver told us two Casualty Officers would meet us at Reagan International Airport. Unfortunately, we had no information about them, so we'd have to locate them once we arrived. As we entered security processing, the Transportation Security Administration attendant paused.

"I recognize who you are, and I'm so sorry for your loss, Mrs. Warner," she told Melissa. "I know you're going to Arlington to bury your son. Please know I will be praying for you, and your family."

Melissa graciously thanked her for her encouraging words. It were as if God were sending angels along the way to support us through this challenging part of our journey.

As we waited for our flight, several strangers approached us to offer their condolences. We were trying to get used to being recognized everywhere we went, and neither Melissa nor I enjoyed being in the limelight. Heath's death was a high-profile media event—for the last three weeks, reporters followed us through the aftermath of Heath's death, the planning of his funeral, the service in Canton, and now his burial at Arlington National Cemetery. Our lives changed dramatically, and not only had we lost Heath, we also were now a Gold Star Family. Being a Gold Star Family has a public side, and we were just learning how to navigate it. We didn't realize our family was now part of America's history—no one prepared us for this, and we didn't have a public relations consultant guiding us. However, Melissa and I were determined to maintain our dignity, so in that effort we tried to be courteous, appreciative, and thankful to all of the kind people we met.

It wasn't too long before boarding, and we quickly found our seats. Chandler sat next to me, Ashton with Melissa. We barely spoke because Heath's burial weighed on us, and once we were airborne my mind began to process I was going to bury my son. This was a flight no parent wants to make, or should have to make. My mind raced between thoughts of our lives with Heath, and what lay ahead of us the following day. I found it hard to believe my son would be buried where valor rests among U.S. presidents, war heroes, and those who paid the ultimate price for freedom.

The plane landed and as we exited into the terminal, Melissa and I looked anxiously for our Casualty Officers. Among strangers and so many different men and women in military uniforms, how would we find them? Fortunately, they carried a sign with our name, and they greeted us kindly. After brief introductions, they helped us gather our baggage.

On our way to the Key Bridge Marriott in Arlington, the Casualty Officers told us they were there to serve us twenty-four-seven during our stay.

"That sounds good to me," I joked. "I'll start with a twelve-pack of Bud Light being sent up to the room!" Though we laughed, I was dimly aware I was already seeking a way to bury the pain.

After checking into the hotel, we took time to relax in our room. Chandler and Ashton wanted to go out to see the memorials, and it wasn't long before some of our relatives called to invite us to see the sights along the National Mall.

But a tour of the Mall would have to wait, because Melissa and I had an interview scheduled with an international news crew at the Iwo Jima Memorial.

During the interview, we shared our pride in our son and talked about what an honor it was to bury him among veterans at Arlington National Cemetery. The interviewer tried to politicize the conversation by asking if we thought his death were in vain. There was a time I would have been infuriated by such an insensitive question—but, now? Unfortunately, I was used to it, and I'm certain reporters have an agenda. "This isn't about the President, or about the war," I responded. "It's about honoring our son. We believed in him, what he was doing, and we are so proud of him." We terminated the interview, and returned to the hotel.

Our Marine escorts, Ryan and Jimmy, arranged for two vans to take my family and relatives to visit the National Mall, and the trip helped relieve our anxiety about Heath's burial service. Ryan and Jimmy knew just where to take us, and what to say. We walked to the Korean War Memorial, the Vietnam Wall, the World War II Memorial, and the Washington Monument before ending up on the steps of the Lincoln Memorial to rest and chat. Before long, midnight was only a few clicks away, and we were on our way back to the hotel.

As we wound down and the boys settled into bed, I reviewed the poem I would read at Heath's grave—I also prepared a note to enclose with a special Christmas ornament, and they were the same our Congressman Ralph Regula would present to President George W. Bush. I wanted the president to know something about my son who gave his life for

our country under his command. I wanted the
president to see my son's face and name, and for him
to know there was a lost and grieving family behind
this casualty.

The next morning, we inched into the day. We
took our time eating breakfast and, as we ate, my
nerves started to get the best of me. The thought of
burying Heath terrified me, and I wasn't sure if I
could go through with it.

I knew I had to call my dear friend who was one
of the first people I contacted after receiving the
news about Heath—I knew she would understand
my pain. She buried two children, so I knew I could
speak as a grieving parent pleading for help from
another.

"It's Scott."

"What's wrong, Scott?"

"I … I can't do this."

"What can't you do?"

"I can't bury him. I'm terrified."

"Why?"

"I can't put him in the ground—I just can't do
it."

"Scott, you have to," she kindly, but firmly
replied. "It's been almost three weeks. Your family
is exhausted, and emotionally drained. You have to
find strength within yourself, and do this not just
you, but for your family, too." I knew she was right,

but it felt so wrong—parents shouldn't bury their children. The entire experience was emotionally pushing me to the brink.

We chatted for a few more minutes before I returned to the hotel room to get ready for the Arlington service. Melissa and I dressed in black velvet suits, and the boys looked so grown up in their suits and ties. When we left the hotel, I was surprised to find the day was bright and sunny with temperatures in the upper sixties—it felt like spring, not mid-December. The beautiful weather took the edge off the darkness I felt inside ... but, I still struggled to find the balance I needed to get through the day.

As visitors, we entered Arlington National Cemetery through the Visitor Center. Today ... today, we entered through formal black iron main gates embellished with gold medallions, representing each branch of the military in honor of the soldiers who lay within. Our lives were now integrally connected to this cemetery—never again would we simply be tourists paying homage to the nation's war heroes.

Our own son would rest in this hallowed ground.

Our Marine Escorts drove us directly to the Administration Building, and staff directed us to a waiting room in the lower level of the building. The simple room was furnished comfortably with seating to accommodate our thirty guests, many of whom were already there. Our U.S. Congressman, Ralph Regula, attended with one of his aides, who is a family friend. It was comforting to see a familiar face in this very unfamiliar place.

When it was time for the burial service, our vehicles lined up to follow the hearse to the grave. My heart was pounding—I was trying to keep myself together, but the thought of burying my son frightened me. I knew he was dead, but I couldn't bring myself to put him in the cold ground, never to be seen again.

The Marine Honor Guard waited beside Heath's grave to provide the final tribute to their fallen brother. We got out of our vehicle, anxiously waiting for the rest of our guests to follow. The Marines marched to the open hearse, faced each other, and precisely aligned themselves to receive this most honored hero. They began to roll out Heath's casket, and Marine officers near the hearse saluted Heath, lowering their hands ever so slowly to their sides while remaining at attention. Melissa and I walked alongside Heath's casket to escort our son to his final resting place, with Chandler and Ashton following us. I couldn't help but glance at Heath's flag-covered casket—it was a beautiful, solemn, and sobering sight. And, even though I wasn't aware, persistent camera clicks reminded me the media was present.

There were two rows of five seats. I sat next to Melissa, Ashton next to me, and Chandler beside him. Our guests sat behind us. As the Marines brought Heath's casket before us, they raised it over their heads, held it briefly, and slowly lowered it to its resting place. The Final Salute. As they lowered the casket, they seamlessly lifted the flag, and two rows of Marines displayed the flag throughout the service.

I gazed across the field of thousands of white marble headstones—deep green Christmas wreaths with bright red bows decorated graves, a solemn reminder Heath would never again celebrate Christmas here on earth. Jets occasionally roared overhead on their approach to Reagan International Airport, and my mind retreated into a private world as I tried to get through the ceremony with dignity.

After the chaplain spoke, I rose to read "Eulogy of the Common Soldier." The poem spoke to my heart, and I could almost hear Heath's voice.

EULOGY OF THE COMMON SOLDIER
by Aaron Seesan

All mortal beings, which God brought forth, die the same.

Where Valor Rests

Man is not exempt
All will inevitably end as the dust from whence we
came
It matters not of age
Do not mourn me if I should fall in a foreign land
Think this of my passing
In a far-off field a finer soil mixed with the foreign
sand
A dust that is American
A dust that laughed, cried, and loved as an
American
On this plot there shall be
A little piece of America, a patch for the free man
Which no oppressor can take
From this soil grows grass shimmering a little
greener
Brilliant emerald ramparts
A Breeze whisping White Poppies with scent a little
sweeter
Flowers towards Heaven
Mourn not my terrible death but celebrate my cause
in life
Viewed noble or not
I would have sacrificed and gave all that I had to
give
Not to make man good
But only to let the good man live.

Somehow, standing before Heath's casket in front of our family and friends, I recited the beautiful poem without any outward sign of tears. Inwardly, though, I was torn apart and crying. My heart broke for Melissa—she bowed her head during the reading, and I can only imagine her heartache. Ashton and Chandler frequently glanced over at us and the casket, and they were uncertain about what to do. As I returned to my seat, Ashton scooted over next to his mother, seeking comfort, and I sat between Chandler and Ashton through the rest of the service. Across the field, the Patriot Guard stood at attention.

The Marine Honor Guard's white gloves used special movements as they smoothed and folded the casket flag reverently, and precisely. The vision of Heath standing at my bed after his death popped into my head—Heath did the exact hand movements, and at the same angle as the Honor Guard. What did it mean?

After folding, the Marine held the flag to his chest, and he began gently patting it, tucking the end of the flag into the fold ever so gently as if holding a baby. Then it swiftly passed down the Marine Honor Guard line to the last man who raised it in the air, then held it to his chest. Then, he handed it off to Colonel Boyle—Colonel Boyle took the flag, and knelt before Melissa.

"On behalf of the President of the United States, the Commandant of the Marine Corps, and a grateful nation, please accept this flag as a symbol of our appreciation for your loved one's service to Country and Corps." Colonel Boyle presented the flag to Melissa, stood up, and gave her a kiss on the cheek. The boys and I leaned forward to see.

I'll never forget what followed after he stood at attention and saluted us—Melissa kept her eyes on him the entire time. He took off his right glove, approached the family, offered his personal condolences, leaned forward, and gave Melissa another hug and kiss on her cheek. She winced in pure pain, holding back a fountain of tears. Photographers captured her shattered expression, and the photo appeared on the front page of many Ohio newspapers. We later learned the picture received honorable mention in a competition for professional photographers.

I don't remember what Colonel Boyle said to the boys and me, but he offered his sincere condolences and appreciation of our family's sacrifice. Other Marines followed Colonel Boyle's lead, taking off their right gloves, and offering their personal condolences. The Marine Honor Guard began to march away in unison, leaving Heath's casket bare and alone on top of his grave, and I knew our final goodbye was shortly upon us.

Following the presentation of the flag, Heath received a twenty-one gun salute. A lone bugler played Taps—*All is well, safely rest. God is near.* Each note stabbed my heart as its haunting, melancholy sound faded into the wind. Something died inside me as I listened to the simple melody, bidding farewell to my son. Family members quietly filed out, and waited for us on the lawn across the street.

And we were left alone with Heath.

With silent tears flowing, my arm was around Melissa as we walked to the coffin to say our final goodbye. I stretched my arms across Heath's casket, and leaned forward to give it one last kiss. One last, gut-wrenching goodbye. My worst fear had become reality, and the grief was unbearable.

Behind us, the boys sat apart. Chandler covered his face, weeping into his hands, while Ashton stared vacantly into the distance. The moment signified what was to become the new norm in our home, each of us separated by our personal grief, trying to cope with it in our own ways.

We were escorted to the lawn, and Colonel Boyle explained to our guests Heath was awarded a Purple Heart Medal for sacrificing his life in the line of duty. Calling Ashton and Chandler forward, Colonel Boyle presented each of the boys with a Purple Heart medal in honor of Heath. Ashton seemed exceptionally excited and he accepted the medal on behalf of his brother, his face lighting up as the Colonel handed the medal to him. I was grateful to Colonel Boyle for honoring our request to present Heath's Purple Heart to his brothers.

I stole a glance across the field one last time to see Heath's casket lowering into the grave.

Later that evening, as we were talking about the day's events at our hotel room, I asked Melissa, "Do you realize the administrators at Arlington never gave us an opportunity to confirm the coffin was actually Heath's? They just brought a coffin out of the hearse, and set it before us."

Melissa thought about it a moment.

"You're right, Scott. But this is Arlington National Cemetery, and I'm sure they had everything in order." I assumed she was right, and I dismissed my concerns.

We returned home on December 13, 2006, nearly three weeks from the day we were notified of Heath's death. We were drained, tired, numb, and despondent—all jumbled in a mess of thoughts and feelings.

We were changed.

10

Raising an American Hero

As we move through life, our lives resemble tumbling dominoes—one event affecting another, connecting each event to the next. I believe God has a specific mission for our lives—a purpose to be accomplished. *Could I have arranged growing up in a conservative home, or becoming friends with my wife's brother in my church youth group? What about attending the same church as Melissa while she was in the midst of her crisis pregnancy? Or, playing blocks on the floor with her baby son? Falling in love with Melissa? Getting married? Adopting Heath?*

I've given it a lot of thought, and I think it's all part of a Master Plan—and God has a plan for me, and he had a plan for Heath. When I think about

raising Heath, I think of one of my favorite songs
"Maria" from *The Sound of Music*. Even though the
song references a girl, the song describes my Heath.
He was his own person, unique in every way.
Gentle. Wild. Riddle. Headache. Child. Flighty.
Darling. Demon. Lamb. Each word brings so many
memories, some funny, some sad, and some warm.
Melissa entrusted me to be Heath's father when he
was still a young child, and I took the responsibility
seriously when I began dating Melissa. I had to think
about the logistics of being a parent, and I had to be
certain I would be the best father to Heath.

Shortly before I asked Melissa out, I bought my
first car, a Pontiac Sunbird.

"You should really think about the car you buy.
You're at the age you could get married, and a two-
door car won't work," my brother Mike told me. But
I just laughed at him—he was so right! I was twenty-
five and within six months of buying my Sunbird, I
was dating Melissa, and I had a car seat in the back
seat of my ride!

Heath was part of our lives from the beginning
of our relationship, and I tried to include him in
everything we did. Melissa carefully balanced being
my girlfriend with being Heath's mother—I vividly
remember visiting Melissa at her home, and my arm
was around her waist. Heath sidled up between us,
pushed me away, and said, "My mommy!" I

immediately understood what was taking place—
Heath knew his mommy was sharing her heart with
someone else, and he didn't like it.

I knelt down and looked him in the eyes.

"Heath, I have an idea. How about if we both
share Mommy?" He paused for a moment, simply
said okay, and we began to forge a family.

I sensed Heath was a kindred soul with a kind
heart and a free spirit—and God placed Heath's
heart and soul into my custody. As Melissa and I
were dating, I had to be careful not to overstep my
boundaries—I wasn't his father yet. However, I
made cautious and gentle suggestions to Melissa
about parenting Heath. It was important for Melissa
to trust me, but I couldn't overstep her as Heath's
mother.

During those early days, I recall Heath cried
frequently. Melissa and I wound up loading his car
seat into the back of my Sunbird and taking him on
drives until he cried himself to sleep. As our dating
relationship continued and it was obvious we were
heading toward marriage, I mentally prepared myself
for the task ahead. I was committed to our
relationship, marrying Melissa, and becoming
Heath's father. I knew it wouldn't be easy, but I also
knew it was the right thing to do.

Although he was biracial, Heath called himself Egyptian. At a young age, Heath discovered he loved books, and he found a book about Egyptians. As he looked at the pictures, he thought his skin color looked like the people in the book, so he referred to himself as Egyptian. However, if you talked to him, he referred to his skin color as white. Melissa and I talked about it, and we decided it was appropriate to talk to him about his skin color—we suggested his skin color was tan. He understood the concept of light and dark, so it was easy to share with him tan was a combination of light and dark colors. He got it, and it seemed to settle the issue in his three-year-old mind.

When we were married, Heath was the ring bearer in our wedding. He looked so handsome in his tuxedo! We looked forward to seeing him carefully balancing the white satin pillow in his hands as he earnestly made his way down the aisle. It wasn't to be, though—his nerves got the best of him, and he ended up in the arms of Uncle Bud throughout the ceremony. He beamed with pride in wedding photos of the three of us together as a new family and, a few years later, when his brother Chandler saw Heath in our wedding photos, he asked, "How did that happen?" We just laughed.

After our wedding, Melissa, Heath, and I lived in Virginia Beach at Regent University where I was attending graduate school. My new four-year-old son was trying to figure out his new family—after all, he was perfectly content living at Melissa's parents' house, with Mom and grandparents always nearby.

I remember lying on the couch, and Heath came up to me—I thought he was going to give me a kiss, but he leaned over and bit my nose! It was clear sharing mommy was harder for him than he anticipated, and he was letting me know he wasn't exactly happy about this new family.

Nonetheless, I wanted to adopt Heath and be a real father to him. So, thanks to friends from graduate school who provided an attorney for us as a wedding gift, I adopted Heath on July 15, 1992. He was no longer Heath Douglas Metzger—he was Heath Douglas Warner! Now, all of us had the same last name, and the birth certificate stated that I, Scott N. Warner, was Heath's father.

_____

While I attended graduate school, Melissa, Heath, and I went to Williamsburg on the weekends. We were so poor we sat on the front porch of Cracker Barrel with a dollar's worth of hot balls. This became one of our weekly rituals, and Heath always looked forward to our time in the quaint town. He liked to look in the stores, and we eventually bought him a colonial tri-corner hat, and toy muzzleloader. Heath loved his new 'uniform' and he marched around the house like a little patriot.

I also took him to Jamestown, Yorktown, and many battlefields from the Revolutionary and Civil Wars. I showed him where the troops lined up, and where ships were positioned in the harbors. He developed an appreciation for our nation's history and, over the years, Heath and I often had interesting discussions about history, or the latest political news.

After graduate school, we moved back to Ohio, and we stayed put throughout Heath's life. He attended Worley Elementary in Canton and, early on, one of Heath's teachers suggested he might have Attention Deficit Hyperactivity Disorder (ADHD), and she recommended we hold him back in kindergarten. Although we suspected this was an issue in his young life, we didn't hold him back. We felt the teacher was inexperienced because it was her first year of teaching, and she was protective of Heath.

As it turned out, it was one decision Melissa and I regretted as Heath grew. He needed that extra year to solidify the foundations of his education and, as time progressed, he struggled with fundamentals, and we began to dread each new school year. After about the third week, the phone calls started and the conferences began.

During his third grade year, Heath came home from school with news.

"Dad, my teacher told me I would never amount to anything."

"I don't want you listening to that teacher," I answered. "She doesn't know what she's saying—I'll take care of it."

I promptly called his teacher at home, hoping Heath misinterpreted her comments.

"Heath came home from school today, and said you were upset with him," I began. "He said you told him he wouldn't amount to anything in his life. I'm sure he misunderstood you, but I want to clarify exactly what was said."

"Well, Mr. Warner, I was frustrated with Heath, and that is what I said to him."

To a third-grader? I decided Melissa and I needed to do more to help our son than simply make a phone call to the teacher. "I will see you at school tomorrow morning with the principal."

And so we met. The teacher was so frustrated, she walked out of the meeting. The principal, school psychologist, and I made a plan to get him through the rest of the school year. Unfortunately, though, the damage was done—the teacher's words pierced his heart.

They haunted him until the day he died.

After graduating from the Marine boot camp, Heath wanted to put on his dress blue uniform, knock on that teacher's classroom door and say, "Do you remember me? I was the student you said wouldn't amount to anything." He wanted to show her she was wrong.

He never did go to see her, but after Heath was killed, Worley Elementary held a special assembly to honor their fallen ex-student. Ashton was a student there, and the principal presented him with a special plaque honoring Worley Elementary war hero Pvt. Heath Warner. The plaque and a framed picture of Heath are still on display in the entrance hallway. The teacher who said Heath's life would never amount to anything walks past it every day, and all I can hope is she realizes the damage she did to a young, impressionable student.

While growing up, Heath struggled to find his place with friends. The churches we attended were predominantly white, and the kids in the youth programs never really embraced Heath. He always felt like an outsider, and he struggled to find his identity. Heath was quirky, often voicing random thoughts or doing random things, and those who knew him just accepted his uniqueness. Over time, his friendships solidified with what we called the 'neighborhood gang'. These kids grew up with our family, and they loved Heath through thick and thin—when we lost Heath, the neighborhood gang stood with us through our darkest moments.

But when Heath was ten, he struggled to find himself. The black students didn't accept him, often referring to him as *White Boy*, and *Oreo*. And when they asked Heath, "Why don't you talk like us?" he responded, "I'm my own person."

It was then he struggled with depression.

He'd go to school, come home, and sleep. His mother and I noticed his behavior and, although he didn't say anything to us, we sensed he was trying to figure out why he looked so different from his parents. We anticipated a discussion about it, and we knew we had to answer his questions about our family.

I walked into his bedroom.

"Heath, you seem to have a lot on your mind," I commented. "Your mother and I want you to know it's okay to talk about any of your questions— whenever you're ready."

"Okay, Dad." I retreated, wondering if he would take me up on my offer.

Moments later, Melissa and I were enjoying a cup of coffee in the kitchen, when Heath came in and sat down. He drew a deep breath, and looked at us nervously. I think he was afraid of hurting our feelings and, at the same time, he wanted his questions answered.

"The kids at school are saying you aren't my parents because you're white," he confessed. "I just need to know the truth."

"We are your parents," Melissa said. "You actually grew in my belly, and your father adopted you." We sensed some relief, but there was more.

"I understand that, but who is my 'real' dad?"

Melissa took charge of the conversation. "Well, Heath, your dad is your real father. A real father is the one who cares about you, and loves you. You want to know who your biological father is …"

She proceeded, choosing her words carefully.

"I don't know who your biological father is—he was a bad man who forced himself on me, and hurt me. But out of this bad thing came something very special and good, and that is you."

Heath just sat there taking it in. "Mommy, I'm sorry that man hurt you," he said as he gave her a big hug,

"Heath, are you okay?" I asked.

"Yes, Dad, I feel a lot better." He gave us each a hug, and went to his room to think about what he just learned. Our conversation seemed to get him through his deep questions, as well as giving him some peace.

But, it's safe to say nothing came easy for Heath. He had to work harder to do more than other kids do at his age in order to achieve what he wanted in life, and Melissa and I encouraged him in everything he did. Throughout grade school, Heath wanted his star on Worley's Wall of Fame for Student of the Month, but it always eluded him. His ADHD was a barrier to his achieving success and, finally, at the end of his fourth grade year he was named to the Wall of Fame.

"Mom! Dad! I did it! I made it on the Wall of Fame!" He beamed a big, beautiful smile.

"Congratulations, Heath! We knew you could do it!" Of course, Melissa and I made a big deal about it because we wanted him to know he was special, and that he could do anything he wanted to do in life.

As our family expanded, first with Chandler in 1992, and then Ashton in 1999, Heath became the best big brother, and his kind, nurturing heart was evident in his care and protection of them. Despite the age difference, Heath and Chandler became best friends, and Chandler was Heath's shadow. He hung out with Heath and the neighborhood gang, and Heath included him in whatever they did, from jumping on the trampoline to break dancing in the basement.

Raising an American Hero

Ashton idolized Heath, and he wanted to be just like his big brother. Heath was very patient with his baby brother—he held him as a baby, and called himself 'brothee', which became Ashton's nickname for Heath. As a teenager, Heath was a big help by helping to care for Ashton, especially since Melissa and I both worked. It was funny, because Heath realized babies were a lot of responsibility, and little children required a lot of work. Heath affectionately called Ashton his birth control—he didn't want the responsibility of being a teenage father!

In his early teen years, Heath took an interest in break dancing. He saw dancers perform, and he decided to teach himself—before we knew it, Heath was busting some moves, and his friends were joining him. His best friends formed a group, the Ground Force Crew, and they began taking lessons at the Living Fountain Dance Company. The Executive Director took notice of Heath, and she asked him to teach break dancing to the youth of Canton. He gained confidence through performing and teaching, and his teaching turned out to be a turning point in his life.

In high school, Heath came into his own as a person. He especially took an interest in foreign languages while taking German and, as a child, Heath loved to research different cultures. He was so inquisitive—somehow, this translated into his love for exotic foods such as octopus, squid, and rare fish. I often wondered, *where did that come from?* We were simple mid westerners, and our foods were Italian and American fare—pasta, pizza, and barbecue.

Heath often talked of traveling to exotic places, especially Japan. Since middle school, Heath's bedroom walls sported posters of Bruce Lee, and soldiers. He often talked about going into the military, and he thought of himself as a modern-day Samurai. I didn't take it seriously, because I chalked it up to his youth. However, we came from a family of military service members—my great grandparents were also Gold Star parents, and they lost their son when he was shot down in the Pacific Campaigns during World War II. As a youth, I didn't comprehend the magnitude of what they lived through, but now I wish they were alive so that I could talk with them.

However, my parents instilled a love for God, family, and country that I translated into my home. On Memorial Day, I made sure to take the boys down to the McKinley Monument in Canton to wave to the veterans, and thank them for their service.

Teaching children about heart issues and values is never easy. I was faithful to raise my family in a Christian home with a love for God, and during Heath's teenage years, there was a sign on our refrigerator that read, *Choices have Consequences.* Every time he left, we would jokingly yell out the door, "Make good choices!" Heath would smile back, "Yes, Mom, and Dad." It was a good laugh! Those were the fun times—but parenting Heath had its challenges.

His first job was bussing tables at a local ice cream shop owned by a neighbor, and a quick walk down the street. He hadn't worked there long when one week I noticed he had an unusual amount of cash in his pocket.

"Heath, where did all that money come from?"

"Oh, it's just tips from bussing. It was a busy weekend."

It seemed a reasonable explanation, so I didn't pursue it. The following week Heath went to work and Melissa and I had to run errands, but when we returned home, Heath was sitting on the back step.

"Why are you home from work so early? Was it a slow night?" I asked.

"Well, not exactly. I got sent home early," he responded, his head hung low.

Sensing something had happened, I asked him about it.

"I stole tips from the waitresses off the tables, and I got caught."

"You did what? What were you thinking?" Melissa and I were not only disappointed with his choice—we were also embarrassed.

I asked, "Are you fired?"

"I don't know. I just got sent home."

The next morning, I called our neighbor. He was gracious, and chalked it up to one of those stupid things teenagers do, and he also mentioned his children made their own stupid decisions.

"Heath is a good kid. It's just one of those things, and I really don't want to fire him."

Melissa and I decided this was a 'teaching' moment, and Heath needed a severe consequence to match what he did. We believed Heath needed to be fired, repay what he stole, and apologize to our neighbor, and the servers. We knew it would be difficult … but Heath called and arranged to atone for his behavior. As parents, it was killing us to do this to Heath—however, this was a matter of the heart, and Heath had to learn. We wanted to make certain he understood there are tough consequences, and he could never do this again.

In time, Heath started working at a local grocery store bagging groceries, and eventually he worked his way up to cashier. He worked there until he left for boot camp after graduation. I worried about his making the same mistake as his first job, but we had to have faith in him he would make the right decision.

And, he did.

"You know, Dad, I'm really thankful you and Mom came down hard on me when I stole those tips. I learned a lesson I never would have learned if I weren't fired. That was really stupid of me, and I'll never do anything like that ever again."

Thank you, God! filled my mind as I realized Heath understood—he was growing up, and bringing maturity into his decision-making process. I felt more confident as a father, and I recognized investing my heart and soul into his development as a young man was paying off.

————————

On September 11, 2001, I was at work listening to a talk radio station, when the radio host announced, "A plane has crashed into one of the Twin Towers in lower Manhattan." In my mind, I pictured a Cessna, misguided in morning fog, crashing into one of the towers. I never imagined the magnitude of the events that were unfolding. Moments later, a reporter was interviewing an eyewitness to the first airliner crashing into the tower, when the interviewee suddenly screamed as a second airliner crashed into the second tower. My first thought was *terrorists*.

My co-workers and I were glued to our radios and computers as we watched the rest of the events unfold. My employer sent us home early—and I didn't have clue how drastically the national tragedy would intimately change our family.

Heath came home from school that afternoon and announced, "I'm going to fight for my country," and he was adamant in his conviction. However, I hoped any conflict arising out of this horrific event would be over by the time he graduated since he was only a freshman. As he finished his high school years at McKinley Senior High, he had one thought on his mind—to serve his country. During his junior year, recruiters called the house on a daily basis in an effort to recruit Heath, and I finally asked them to stop calling. I wanted Heath to have the rest of his junior year to consider his options.

That worked until the beginning of his senior year when the phone began ringing again, and Heath decided he wanted to become a Marine. I invited the recruiter to our home, and asked him to bring the book with all the MOSs (Military Occupational Specialty) for which Heath was qualified. I sat on the ottoman, Heath was on the couch next to the recruiter, and Melissa sat on the loveseat. The recruiter went page by page, explaining all of the positions for which Heath was qualified. However, Heath just sat there shaking his head no with his arms folded, saying "Infantry." He wouldn't settle for anything else.

Our kindhearted son was going to become a warrior.

Melissa and I felt we had no other option but to support him. We signed the paperwork for him to register into the delayed entry program of the United States Marine Corp. The delayed entry program allowed Heath to enlist as an inactive reservist while in his senior year of high school, and Heath vowed to be one of America's best—a Marine.

While in the delayed entry program, Heath began attending the weekly training of upcoming recruits in advance of boot camp. For his entire senior year, we prepared for Heath's departure. It was a scary thought knowing our son was training to go to war in Iraq. At his graduation, Heath entered the Canton Civic Center as a Marine, making a sharp left turn into the row where he was to sit. The entire family and his friends laughed!

Knowing Heath was going to war, I went all out on his graduation party—in the back of my mind, I thought, *this could be the last party I ever throw for him*, and we had it catered at our home.

The summer after his graduation ended too soon, and in August of 2005, we met at the MEPS center to send Heath off to boot camp. Our nerves were on edge as we watched Heath sign his contract, and then recite his Oath of Service to his country. As we waited for the bus to Paris Island, we took family photos. Heath wasn't nervous at all—in fact, he was so excited he couldn't wait to get on that bus! And when it finally arrived, he gave each of us a hug, and we said our final "I love you" to Heath. He peered out the window, smiling, and waving to us as the bus departed and pulled out onto the road. It was a stark contrast to other families who were crying, and following the bus as it pulled out.

Now it was Heath's turn to fly, and he was ready to soar.

Heath was a deeply thinking person—on his MySpace page he quoted Bruce Lee:

"Life's battles don't always go to the stronger or faster man, but, sooner or later, the man who wins is the man who thinks he can."

Heath realized life was hard work, but he was determined to become a Marine, and nothing was going to stop him. He also wrote:

Spend some time with me, and you'll know who I am!"

Heath was a special, unique person, and those of us who knew him, loved him and appreciated his uniqueness. On November 18, 2005, we met Heath on the parade grounds of Paris Island, South Carolina. This time there were tears of joy and happiness as he ran into his mother's arms, picked her up, and gave her a giant hug. We were celebrating a dream come true for our son—I was proud watching him march as a Marine on the parade grounds.

Prior to Heath's leaving for Iraq we were spending some precious time together, and Heath paused for a second.

"Dad, I want to thank you for being my Dad. Thank you for giving me a name, and a family."

"Heath, it's been an honor and privilege to be your Dad."

I cared for the gift God had entrusted in my hands—a precious life. With God's grace and through the many difficulties in life, I invested my heart and soul into raising Heath, and I felt I had done all I could do in the raising of an American hero.

11

Collateral Damage

We arrived home from Washington, D.C. on December 13, 2006, around eight o'clock in the evening. Once we unloaded the van, I decided to 'de-funeralize' the house—it smelled like a funeral home because of the scores of flowers we received. I threw the dying floral arrangements into the trash, went outside to pull in the flags from the street, and remove the banner from the front fence. I couldn't handle the focus on death, and I wanted our house to have some sense of normalcy.

"Scott, why did you take everything down? I wasn't ready for everything to be taken away!"

"I'm sorry, Honey. I just couldn't stand looking at any of this for another day. But, you're right—I should have asked you first."

I should have considered Melissa's feelings, but my grief overwhelmed me, and I didn't realize it at the time, but I was developing a pattern of focusing on my own sorrow at the expense of my family. Melissa and the boys were doing the same. Our family was broken and, as a Dad, I couldn't fix it. Grief consumed us, and we were unable to seek solace in each other. In fact, it took years for us to begin sharing our feelings, and grieving together.

The next day, we awakened to an empty house—no family, guests, or any of the business associated with Heath's funeral.

Nothing but silence.

Normally, the sounds of music CDs filled the house, but, today, no one wanted to listen to music. We didn't even know what to say to each other, and we aimlessly wandered around the house all day. At night, we slept together on our queen-sized bed.

It wasn't long after we got home that men from Heath's unit began to call, but I was too grief-stricken to talk with anyone from Iraq, so I ignored them. But they continued to leave messages, pleading for me to return their calls.

Finally, Melissa set me straight. "Scott, I think you need to talk to these boys," she said gently. "They're obviously hurting, and they want to talk to you. They're hurting just as we are, but they don't have anyone to comfort them in Iraq."

Though I knew it would be painful, I answered the next call, and a voice introduced himself as one of Heath's closest friends. The words poured from him in a torrent of grief as he described the emptiness he felt without Heath.

Then, another call. A young service member spoke of his friendship with Heath and how they watched out for each other. He especially missed Heath's insights during their Bible studies together—these two young men were the Christians Heath mentioned to us in his only letter from Iraq!

After speaking with them, I was determined these two boys would come home alive, so we began communicating regularly through email. They shared their hardships, sadness, and heartaches.

"There is a time to grieve," I told them, "but, right now, you need to focus on doing your jobs each day. Think about your parents who are anxiously awaiting your homecoming to love on you. You have to live! Be strong! Be courageous!"

I prayed for them. Whatever it took, I made myself available to get them through the horrors of war. There was no escaping the long-term consequences of war—pain was, and always will be, a part of their lives.

But I had to focus on my family's needs, as well—and my family was lost. Tears were always near the surface, and none of us had much energy.

As Christmas approached, we were unable to face the sacred holiday, and we couldn't bring ourselves to haul out the decorations. Thankfully, friends put up our Christmas tree and decorated the house, and Aunt Harriet took Melissa Christmas shopping for the boys. However, no Christmas music filled the house, and the usual aroma of baking cookies was absent.

There was nothing but raw pain.

Our Christmas Eve tradition was to celebrate at my cousin's house—normally a time to reminisce with family and friends, we now dreaded the annual pilgrimage. Nonetheless, we dragged ourselves to the car and did our best to honor the holiday.

That night, I filled four Christmas stockings instead of five. Tears poured down my cheeks, and dripped onto the hearth as I imagined Christmas morning without Heath. As a little boy, Heath joyfully tore open his presents faster than we could hand them to him. Last year, our three sons sat next to each other on the couch, laughing with glee as they opened their gifts. Only two boys would share the couch tomorrow. Only two boys would dig through their stockings for treasures.

Ashton and Chandler slept in later than usual on Christmas morning. Ashton, who still believed in Santa Claus, shrieked when he saw the gifts under the tree, but the rest of us were numb. I was looking forward to going over to Doug's house for the distraction, but during Christmas dinner, I found myself wanting to crawl into a hole and sleep the day away. Spending Christmas at Melissa's parents' home was our usual tradition, but that would never happen again. Reminders of Heath were everywhere, triggering tears and sorrow without warning.

We had to create new traditions.

"What do you think about going to Disney World to escape after Christmas?" I asked Melissa. I already spoke to a travel agent to plan the last-minute trip, and I was thrilled when Melissa agreed getting away would be good for the boys. So we prepared to spend the week between Christmas and New Year's on an escape to the Magic Kingdom.

As we were packing to leave, there was a rap on the door.

"I'll get it!" I yelled to Melissa. A package was placed on the wicker table on the front porch, and I thought someone had dropped off a gift. Then I opened the door, and what I saw hit me like a punch in the stomach—I couldn't breathe. There sat a pile of boxes, stacked six, or seven high—our Christmas presents for Heath, shipped back to us from Iraq as part of his personal effects.

"Scott, what's wrong?" Melissa asked in alarm when she saw my face. Speechless, I pointed to the door, managing to croak, "Look." Cautiously,

Melissa peered outside, then turned to me, stricken. We hoped Heath had the chance to open his Christmas gifts—the Christmas tree with our pictures on it, the Christmas stocking with our special messages.

But, he didn't. Melissa's face crumpled, and I held her tightly, blinded by my own tears as she sobbed into my chest.

Chandler took the boxes into the basement.

At the time, I was grateful he did what he thought was best to help his mother and father—I never realized his own grief was overwhelming him.

We arrived at Disney World the following day, and we stayed at our favorite resort. As we entered our room, a Mickey Mouse vase filled with flowers greeted us. There was a note from our travel agent wishing us a great trip, knowing the sadness we were walking through in our lives.

Disney World was decorated for Christmas, holiday garland arched along the many buildings, and the lights added to the festive spirit. However, no matter how hard we tried, we were simply going through the motions.

It was a relief to get back to the hotel, and hop in the pool for a quick dip. As Ashton and I were swimming, I looked up to the sky, and an airplane was sky writing *God Loves You,* which was followed by a big smiley face—I grabbed my camera and, luckily, I captured the photos!

Thank you, God! I needed that! raced through my mind as I looked at the gentle, puffy letters. I knew God was saying, "I'm here, Scott. Hang in there."

We celebrated New Year's Eve at the Boardwalk, and we welcomed 2007. As we stood in the midst of all the happy people, I looked at Melissa, Chandler, and Ashton, wishing them a Happy New Year, but, in my heart, I thought, *Dear Jesus, please help us get through this next year.*

One of my favorite memories of the trip was how silly the boys were with me. I couldn't sleep without medication, and once I took the medication I was knocked out. So … Chandler and Ashton decided to have some fun with my 'condition'. While I was sleeping, they put Melissa's bra on me, covered me in glow sticks, and took pictures of me! Of course, they were laughing all the while, and it was to my surprise the next morning to see all of the silly pictures on my cell phone!

Then it was time to go home. Heath's birthday was the day we returned—January 2, 2007—the day he would have turned twenty. We arrived late in the evening, and we ignored thinking and talking about his birthday. Each of us was painfully aware there wouldn't be any more birthday cakes or cards for Heath.

It was over.

Fortunately, the neighborhood gang was our saving grace—they moved in, and Guitar Hero became the game of choice. We spent our evenings playing the new video sensation—Melissa and I were like the crazy parents on You Tube and, for some reason, the silliness of our battles got us through our long days and nights. Ashton played *Freebird* repeatedly—it was his way of remembering his hero brother, and finding his way through his grief.

Our funeral director told us our first year would be hard. You have to go through all of the first experiences without your loved one—your first day, your first week, your first month, your first winter, spring, summer and fall, your first of all the holidays, your first loved one's birthday, culminating with the first anniversary of your loved one's death. She also told us the second year would be as difficult as the first, and the numbness fades, only to be replaced by the pain of reality.

She was so right. Grieving the loss of Heath is the hardest work I've ever done, and it is the same for my family. It's not only hard because of the grief itself, but because it was a war death—a Muslim extremist murdered our son by blowing him up.

Each time we heard of a new casualty on the news, we relived Heath's death. When your son or daughter dies as an American Hero, your life changes forever—first by the loss and, second, because your family is now part of American history. Our son's name is memorialized throughout the country on monuments, and he's buried at Arlington National Cemetery where he lies in honor with Presidents and military heroes from the past, and present. He could have chosen any other path for his life, but he chose to give his life for freedom.

No one prepared us for what was ahead. We were thrust into a public spotlight without any help from a public relations consultant, and we were on our own to learn on the fly, steeped in gut-wrenching grief.

On January 4, 2007, we tried to return to our old lives. The boys went back to school, and Melissa and I returned to work. Unfortunately, it didn't go well for any of us—Melissa began to receive phone calls from their schools.

"Hello, Mrs. Warner, this is Worley Elementary. Ashton is crying, and he says he feels sick. We have him in the clinic, and he's asking for you to pick him up."

"OK. Thank you for calling. I'll be there as soon as I can."

"Hello, Mrs. Warner? This is Leighman Middle School. Chandler is in the clinic with a bad headache. Can you pick him up?"

"Thank you for calling. I'll be there as soon as I can."

And on it went. Melissa had to leave work to tend to the boys, and eventually it got to the point she had to quit her job in order to help the boys get through the day. She eventually had to attend school with Ashton, and sit with him to get him through his days. This led to volunteering as an aide for Ashton's teacher and, after two years, the school hired Melissa as a teacher's assistant for Canton City Schools.

In mid-January, we received a call from our Marine Casualty Officer.

"Hello, Mr. Warner, we received Heath's personal effects from Hawaii and Iraq. I'd like to set a date to deliver them to you."

We set a date for the delivery, and I dreaded the task. I ended up taking the day off work, and with Melissa at my side, Heath's belongings were returned home—tears spilled as we went through the inventory sheet."

"Heath's iPod is missing. So are his camera, and Nintendo game system."

"I'm sorry sir, but we recovered everything in his belongings." Later, we found out it's not uncommon for other service members to go through the deceased's personal effects, and take items.

When Ashton returned home from school that afternoon, he went down into the basement and saw Heath's belongings.

He lost it.

It was the first time his grief punched him in his gut, and it was the beginning of a painful journey. The vacant stares at Heath's viewing, funeral, and burial were gone—his eyes were now filled with pain, and it was beyond his ability to cope. His meltdowns were very hard to deal with, and attempting to juggle the balance of a child whose young mind isn't equipped to handle and process emotions is difficult. Ashton screamed, threw tantrums, and cried hysterically—and it was pushing our emotions to extremes. I knew I had to do something to help my family.

"Melissa, where is that folder the Casualty Officers left us? There has to be something to help us find help for us, and the boys."

"Check in your office to see if it's with the notebook you kept of the funeral details."

Sure enough, I located the folder and quickly flipped through it. *There has to be something in here about where we can get help*, I thought as I felt a brief sense of panic. Finally, I found a brochure about TAPS (Tragedy Assistance Program for Survivors) which is an organization to help the families of fallen heroes.

There was an 800 number on it, and I called immediately. The person who answered was very kind, took down necessary information, and told me I would receive a call from one of the TAPS staff.

That's when I met Stephanie. She's a fantastic spokesperson for TAPS and, for the first time, I felt a sense of relief. I told her about our family, our loss, and our realization that we were at a loss to help Chandler and Ashton. My conversation with Stephanie was the beginning of a long-term relationship with TAPS, and I learned peer-to-peer support is the foundation for healing. We immediately received resources in the mail, and we found useful information for our family. Stephanie also recommended we attend the National Conference in Washington D.C. over the Memorial Day weekend, 2007. Melissa and I were ecstatic, and we immediately registered for the conference. We couldn't wait for May to arrive!

In the midst of our early grieving, we began to attend the first of many dedications and memorials that became a part of our lives. First, a nameplate was placed at the Canton Memorial Civic Center by the Canton Marine Corp McKinley Detachment, which is comprised of Marine veterans. Recognition of Gold Star families followed in March, and it was the first time since Heath's funeral service I was asked to speak publicly. Emotionally, I wasn't ready to speak, but my heart told me that I must. I felt compelled to defend Heath's death, proclaim the successes our troops were making, and be a voice for those who could no longer speak for themselves— fallen troops, service men and women who were fighting for freedom, and other Gold Star Families. I contacted Heath's Commanding Officer by email and asked him to share, firsthand, the successes taking place in Iraq.

"The very area where Heath was killed is now pacified. Because of your son's effort, Iraqi citizens can walk the streets that had been scenes of hostile gunfire. Children can play safely, as adults go to the markets. Freedom isn't free. It requires the highest cost, the blood, sweat, and tears of our loved ones.

The speech went very well, and I received a standing ovation from a crowd of a thousand people. It was then I realized I had a public platform, and I could make a difference if I used it correctly. I thanked God for making it through successfully.

Collateral Damage

In April, Heath's unit returned from Iraq, and it proved to be a bittersweet homecoming—we wished we could have been there to welcome him home alive, but we were thankful for those who were greeted with fanfare, hugs, and kisses from their wives, husbands, children, and parents.

Twenty-three Marines didn't make it.

———————

Before we went to Hawaii, we arranged to visit Heath's grave for the first time. We hadn't seen his headstone, and we wanted to be as close to him as possible. Burying Heath far away from home was a hard choice, because it meant in order to visit his grave, it was a destination visit—we needed to make hotel arrangements, and pay for food, and gas.

Our pass allowed us through the main gate and, as we entered, I wasn't sure where to go.

"Scott, don't turn there, I think the name of the drive is York."

I navigated a few more roads, turned left on York, and drove to the last row of graves. As we got out of the car, I was amazed to see the row in which Heath was buried was filled in, and a new row started at the other end.

We walked up to the grave as a family.

There was a flower arrangement from another Gold Star family who knew it would be comforting for us to see a fresh flower arrangement next to Heath's headstone. *You're not alone. Thinking of you,* the card read.

"Mommy? Is this where Heath is buried?" Ashton asked.

"Yes, Honey— this is your brother's grave."

Ashton sat with us, and he had his drawing pad. Melissa and I sat on Heath's grave with a blanket underneath us, and our eyes filled with tears—we tried, probably unsuccessfully, to control our emotions in front of the boys. Chandler didn't say a whole lot and after a short time, he asked for the keys to the van.

Shortly after our arrival, a kind woman approached us.

"Are you Private Heath's parents?" We nodded.

"My name is Holly, and I've been looking forward to meeting you."

This was our first meeting with our new friend whom we affectionately refer to as, 'Arlington Holly'. Holly is a local florist who made the lovely flower arrangement for Heath's grave, and she's the unofficial caretaker of Section 60—that means she's the caretaker of Heath's grave.

"Daddy, look what I drew!" Ashton handed me his drawing pad—it was a picture of Heath's gravestone, and underneath it the phrase, *my brother is a hero.* I showed it to Melissa, and with tears in her eyes she said, "You're right, Honey. Your brother is a hero."

Grief stabbed at us as we turned our backs to his grave, and headed back to the van. Before we left, I hugged his headstone and laid my head on the top of it, kissing the cool, smooth surface.

"Goodbye, Heath. We'll back soon." And with that, we left with Holly's homemade cookies, and returned home.

Hawaii was next.

The two service members who were Heath's friends and Christian mates were to be our escorts for the week, and they were to pick us up at Honolulu National Airport. We communicated often, and we couldn't wait to meet them at luggage pick up—there was no mistaking them!

"Hi, Mr. Warner! I'm Joseph, and this is J.R. It's so great to meet you!" We exchanged excited greetings and hugs, and I was so thankful they made it back to Hawaii alive.

Melissa and the boys introduced themselves, and we talked as we waited to pick up our luggage—

then it was off to Denny's for a midnight breakfast. It was a blast, and we laughed for hours! But, by then we were beat, and we arranged to meet up the following day so they could take us to Heath's base. Visiting Heath's base was, again, bittersweet. We walked the places Heath spent his last days alive, and it was an emotional time for all of us as we met the members of his unit. We spent the day together, and Joseph and J.R. asked if they could spend the week with us at our hotel room. Of course, we said yes. It was the right decision, and we bonded as we spent time together. We put the cushions from the couch on the floor, and they used a sitting chair with an ottoman for a bed. We talked about anything and everything, and it was kind of funny—being with them, I felt a connection with Heath. Without them, I couldn't have made it through the week ahead.

The families of the fallen were flown to Kaneohe Bay for two ceremonies. The first was the presentation of the Hawaii Medal of Honor, and the second was the memorial on the base with Heath's unit. The memorial was a turning point for my grief—unfortunately, it was a turn for the worse. I found the ceremonies to be more than I could bear, and as the initial numbness wore off, long-term pain became my constant companion.

During the presentation of the Hawaii Medal of Honor, I received Heath's medal on behalf of the family. As I sat with the other Gold Star families, a young war widow with her baby sat by me. While I played with the baby, holding her on my lap, it hit me—this baby will never know her father. I began to realize the collective pain present among these families. The floodgates opened, and tears flowed—I couldn't stop crying.

J.R.'s sister, Erica, was sitting to my right.

"Scott, you have to pull yourself together!"

"I'm trying, Erica, but I can't!"

As they read each name, a bell tolled, and we were to walk across the stage for the presentation of the medal, as well as pictures with the state's governor and other dignitaries. When they read Heath's name, I proudly walked across the stage, barely holding myself together.

As unbelievable as it is, the memorial ceremony at the base was harder to endure. As we arrived, Joseph and J.R. introduced us to the commanding officers of Heath's unit. Prior to our trip, I sent an email to one of his commanding officers requesting him to bring me sand from Iraq. After introductions, another officer joined us, and he handed me a chewing tobacco container sealed with tape. *Sand – Iraq* was scrawled on the container, and it reminded me of the scene from the movie, *Saving Private*

Ryan, when the soldier collected dirt from the various countries in which he was fighting. While in Hawaii, I also collected white sand from Kanohoe Bay—I added it to my collection of sand from Iraq, and earth from our home in Canton. I now had the ground Heath's feet touched from each part of his life, which I keep at my home office.

As we took our seats for the memorial service, I could barely look across the tarmac of the base. The beautiful backdrop of the Hawaiian Islands, and the crystal blue water of the bay silhouetted the four platoons that comprised Heath's unit from Iraq. They stood in formation in front of us, and encircled in front of the Marines were twenty-three rifles, boots, and helmets with dog tags hanging on them.

The service was as much for the families as it was for the Marines from Heath's unit. One of the most moving moments was watching those brave young men and women kneeling in front of their fallen friend's memorial, sobbing. Standing behind at attention, their friends choked back tears.

When it was our turn, I was reluctant to approach the memorial for Heath. I didn't know what to do—I held his dog tags in my hands, and it seemed like a surreal scene from a movie. After the ceremony, we were presented with a brick that bore Heath's name, rank, and date of death. It was a replica of a brick placed at the Statue of Iwo Jima at

Kaneohe Bay. I asked if Heath's brick were placed at the Iwo Jima Memorial.

"Mr. Warner, we can take you to see it." With that, Joseph and J.R. guided us to the memorial site.

Emotion flooded my soul as I stared at the bricks honoring every Marine who was killed in combat from WWII to the current wars. It was another honor that our hero son was part of the history of the Island Warriors. I circled the memorial slowly, trying to take in all of the names and dates.

All I could think about was lost lives.

As soon as we returned to our hotel room, I called Tom Seesan, and he could tell immediately that something was wrong.

"Hi, Scott—is everything okay? Are you in Hawaii?"

"I'm sitting on the balcony of our hotel, and we just got back from the memorial service. I can't take this—it's too hard. I'm looking at the most beautiful sights of the island, but I can't stop crying."

Tom listened, and he tried to help me get myself together. As much as I tried, however, I could barely keep my emotions in check around the family, and it was becoming more difficult as the number of days from Heath's death increased.

I was falling apart.

When we got home, Julie and Jerry Ramey came over to check on us—they brought Kentucky Fried Chicken, and we discussed how things went in Hawaii. I showed them the Hawaii Medal of Honor, and my souvenirs from the memorial service. I was thankful for their visit, and it helped me recognize I wasn't alone.

———————

We couldn't wait! The drive to Washington for our first TAPS Conference seemed to take forever, and the boys' "Are we there yet?" coupled with, "I'm bored," broke our silent thoughts. We arrived at the Double Tree in Crystal City late in the evening, and the following day we planned to register the boys for Good Grief Camp.

Shortly after breakfast and once we had the boys registered, we took them to their respective locations—the conference allowed them to separate from their parents during the day, and each paired with his new 'best buddy' who was an active duty service member, and mentor.

Melissa and I registered for the adult portion of the conference, and we were nervous—we were overwhelmed by all of the mothers, fathers, adult siblings, wives, and fiancées of loved ones in one location.

Over that weekend, we met new friends who knew the pain we felt in our hearts. It was the first time I could remove the mask I wore in everyday life, and be myself—a bereaved father. We related without any pretense, or fear, of being judged. I remember looking across the three hundred guests at the evening dinner on Saturday night, and all I could think about was, *look at all this pain in one place.* I couldn't help but think of other families across America who weren't there—yet they needed to be.

That weekend, I met the founder of TAPS, and she's a source of inspiration and support to so many hurting people across America. She's a dear friend of the Warner family, and she walks this painful journey with us.

In reality, after the Marine Casualty Officers left our lives, the government abandoned us. They left us to figure how to survive this tragedy on our own—all I can say is I hated it when the TAPS conference ended. I didn't want to go home, and neither did the rest of my family.

The TAPS organization had a huge impact on our family, and Melissa and I eventually became peer mentors for new grieving families because peer-to-peer support is the best method for helping other

Gold Star Families. I honestly don't know how our family would have made it without TAPS.

As time droned on, my depression escalated. The loneliness and darkness was like an anchor, preventing me from moving forward, and in July of 2007, I finally began counseling with a psychiatrist in an effort to find relief. In order to be functional, I had to rely on anti-depressants, anxiety medications, and sleeping pills. My returning to work was especially difficult, because my employer lined the hallway with newspaper clippings surrounding our son's death. When I returned to work, one of my coworkers presented the posters, telling me they put them on the outside of the cubicles of our department.

More life in the fishbowl.

I couldn't focus, and there were days I only stared at my computer. Occasionally, I cried at my desk, and I found myself becoming easily overwhelmed. It was during this time our department went through an organizational change. I struggled to keep up with my work when we lost a financial analyst position, and the powers that be expected me to step up, which only added to my stress. They expected a separation between my work life and personal life, and the professional relationship became more contentious and adversarial over time.

I didn't know what to do.

During my next visit with my psychiatrist, I told him what was happening, and I was afraid my job was on the line—he recommended I consult with an attorney.

My employer took my solid nine years of excellent performance, and reduced me to a chronic problematic employee. My performance records don't reflect their assertions, and if I hadn't seen it in writing, I wouldn't have believed it.

"Warner cannot avoid productivity, performance, or leave eligibility requirements simply because his son died."

Really? My supervisor's and company's lack of understanding of grief, complicated bereavement, and Post Traumatic Stress Disorder is most evident by their referring to the Department of Defense recognition of the Gold Star Family, as the 'Gold Medal Families' organization. In fact, they stated, "He is very involved with an organization called 'Gold Medal Families', and the organization 'TAPS'. In other words, Mr. Warner has so many personal activities, he has little time, or attention to devote to performing his work ..." The Gold Star Family, and TAPS (Tragedy Assistance Program

Services for Survivors) organizations are support organizations for surviving families—neither are social clubs.

For the first time, the manner in which I was treated was documented—it was clear I was an inconvenience. The words, *simply because his son died* haunts, sickens, and angers me. My son sacrificed his life for freedom—freedom for families to live in a safe America, to enjoy life with their families, and even for businesses to operate and employ Americans. Instead, we're witnessing the corruption sparked by greed that is responsible for tanking many of our major corporations, as well as the banking, financial, and housing markets. My family is one of over five thousand families suffering resulting from the wars in Iraq, and Afghanistan. Gold Star Families pay the ultimate price for freedom, and the cost is the blood, sweat, and tears of children, mothers, fathers, brothers, and sisters.

I call these wars the 'un-wars'. Unless you have a loved one who is in the service, or you have lost a loved one in a war, Americans go about their business as usual. I find it very arrogant that companies across America take the position the war will not touch their employees. I challenge companies to consider how they will treat their employee who loses a son, or daughter, due to combat, training, or suicide related to war. For the surviving military families, their lives don't go back to the way they were. Initially, it seemed as if everyone supported the troops when the war first started after 9/11, but as time passed, people went back to business as usual. Unlike wars of the past, the average American hasn't sacrificed because of these wars. For example, in World Wars I and II, all Americans were touched in some way.

The anniversary of Heath's death loomed in the fall of 2007. A melancholy feeling mixed with deep sadness began to fester at the end of August and, in retrospect, that was the last time we saw him alive. I couldn't help but remember all of the last memories we had of Heath—our last visit, phone calls, emails, and texts.

We couldn't bear another sad Thanksgiving— our annual holiday tradition of having family and friends visit was over.

"Melissa, we need to do something different to escape."

"What are you thinking?"

"How about Disney again?"

She liked the idea, and when we asked the boys, they immediately said yes. With that, I made the arrangements and we were off for a long weekend at Disney World!

But all I could think about was Heath's being officially dead for one year. Visions of the Marine Casualty Officers entering our house filled my head, and Melissa was thinking the same thing. We tried to minimize any thoughts of death with Chandler and Ashton, but how do you dodge the elephant in the room? Somehow, we managed to do exactly that— but ignoring and burying pain deep within your heart is dangerous, and unhealthy, in the long term.

But, we made it. We made it through our first year, and I could only hope things would get better.

12

Creating a Legacy

I didn't want Heath to be forgotten.
Making certain his name remains on the lips of
his family, friends and colleagues turned into an
obsession, and no matter how hard I tried to keep my
life in balance, it spiraled out of control. My
obsession that Heath needed an enduring legacy
permeated my mind, heart, and soul—honoring my
son, and remembering a hero became my top, and
only, priority.

Although Heath isn't physically with us, we feel
his presence each day, and I know his life can still
touch others. My mind raced with ideas for his
legacy, but I had no idea about how to bring my
obsession to reality. A friend suggested a bucket list
approach, and it seemed like a good idea. Before I
knew it, I had several viable ideas, and I figured I
could take them one by one: scholarship, memorial

website, hero car, annual fundraiser (5K race, annual dinner), Freedom Award, write a book, public speaking, and the Ohio Medal of Honor.

And so I began a new journey.

Some of the projects progressed easily, while others remain a slow process requiring time, care, self-sacrifice, and patience. Initially, we established the Private Heath Warner Memorial Endowment Fund through the Stark Community Foundation. At the time of Heath's death, we asked for donations to be made to the Stark County Pregnancy Center, or to the Private Heath Warner Memorial Fund established by a caring neighbor.

We used donations for seed money to set up an endowment fund through the Stark Community Foundation. This made sense to us on several levels: first, the Stark Community Foundation was well established, and well respected in the community. We knew donors could be certain their investment in Heath's legacy would be used wisely. Second, it took the burden of administrating a non-profit organization off Melissa and me.

As we discussed the benefits of the endowment fund, we were excited to give back to the community—our goal was to establish a legacy of helping our community memorialize fallen troops, fund programs that build confidence in children, assist single mothers, and help families of fallen troops.

For the fund to become a permanent endowment fund, we had to reach a specific dollar amount. It appeared a daunting task, but we believed over time it could happen. And, once the permanent endowment was secure, we knew Heath would have a legacy that will last throughout our lifetime. Of course, my desire is for his brothers, and their families to continue to honor their brother. So, I knew I needed to create new avenues for promoting, and raising funds for the endowment.

We met Paul after Heath's death—he owned a web design business, and I asked him to help me create Heath's website. A friendship quickly developed as we worked through the purposes of the website:

- to honor Heath's life and sacrifice,
- to centralize, and archive the historical information of his life,
- to link with Heath's friends, as well as new friends, about the latest events celebrating his life, and
- to continue his legacy by promoting the endowment fund.

Paul's work was meticulous, and soon we had a draft of the website: www.pvtheatheathwarner.com.

I was thrilled with Paul's work the first time I visited the site—the photo of Heath with an American flag backdrop, and the phrase:

He died thinking of us, we live thinking of him
Pvt. Heath Warner
January 2, 1987 – November 22, 2006

exceeded my expectations, and I couldn't wait to show Melissa.

"Melissa, you have to see this! I have a draft of Heath's website from Paul!" I opened my laptop and clicked on the link.

"Scott, this is amazing! I love this!" Melissa's reaction mirrored my own—and we knew we were on the right track. The website included photographs of Heath's life, and video clips from the events of Heath's funeral, and memorials. It was the first tangible memorialization completed for Heath.

I prepared a press release and submitted it to various news and media organizations, and our story published in the Akron Beacon Journal on September 14, 2007.

A year ago on Sept. 11, Marine Pvt. Heath Warner left Hawaii for Iraq. About 10 weeks later, the 19-year-old Canton native was killed in a roadside bombing in Iraq.

This year, his family is memorializing him on a website that was launched in late August, www.pvtheathwarner.com.

"I don't want people to forget about who Heath was," said his father, Scott Warner.

The family also has set up an endowment fund through the Stark Community Foundation in Heath's name to keep his legacy alive.

The news article was one of my first, and I was excited to see ideas coming to life that were only thoughts on my bucket list. It gave us peace to know we were creating a legacy for Heath.

To create an annual fundraiser for the endowment fund, we created the Running to Remember, Pvt. Heath D. Warner Memorial 5K Run, and Family Fun Walk.

People asked if Heath were a runner, and why we chose a 5K run. No, Heath wasn't a runner, but I am. Like the website, it was just an idea in my head, and I wasn't too sure if it could actually happen. I wasn't certain if I had the emotional strength to pursue this project—however, I believe if you take a step and a door opens, keeping walking through the door. That simple thought keeps me moving forward.

Having been a participant in the Ohio Subway Challenge Series (the premiere racing series in

Northeast Ohio), I wanted Heath's race to be part of the series. For one thing, I knew it would lend credibility to the race. I initially met with the series owner and we talked about it, but he seemed skeptical about my establishing the race. Maybe he thought I was too emotionally invested in it to make it happen—I don't know. After our initial meeting, though, I prepared a business plan for the race, and pitched the idea again for a Memorial Day 5K Run. He liked the plan, and the Running to Remember, Pvt. Heath Warner 5K Memorial Run became a reality.

To be honest, preparing for the race was a challenging task. Fortunately, I was able to form a committee that connected with Melissa and me— they were kind, caring, and patient. Our goal was to organize and run, a top-notch event—we didn't want anyone to realize it was a first-year race. We scheduled our inaugural race for Memorial Day, May 26, 2008.

As race day approached, I held my breath hoping the weather would cooperate with the event—the forecast called for rain. I said a quick prayer in the morning as I was putting up the mile markers signage at five-thirty in the morning. *Dear God, please let the rain hold off until after the race.* I entrusted it into His hands, trusting all would work out as we anticipated.

The opening ceremony began under overcast, grey clouds with some slight sprinkles that quickly dissipated. I looked across a crowd of four-hundred-and fifty participants, and I was humbled and honored our community was supporting us, and remembering Heath. I teared up as the song, *American Soldier* played—Chandler and Ashton lead the Pledge of Allegiance, and Melissa read a list of fallen soldiers who were killed in action in the Iraq, and Afghanistan wars.

Finally, with a blast of the air horn, the runners were off, and I couldn't believe it! All of our hard work came together in a well-executed, honoring event, and I couldn't help but think of Heath in Heaven looking down, smiling, and shaking his head. "Dad, no way!" he'd say. Heath was such a simple, shy person, and he wouldn't have believed the outpouring of love and support.

After the race, our family was thrilled to award the first cash donation through the Living Fountain Dance Company—it was to help a young professional pursue his or her career. We were honored to donate to the organization, because Heath was a break-dancer with the Living Fountain Dance Company, and now we had the opportunity to present an award to an aspiring dancer who danced with Heath. It was appropriate the first award we presented was part of Heath's life, and I hope it's one of many we'll be able to do to help other people.

———————

In August 2007, Melissa and I approached State Senator Kirk Schuring about creating an official award recognizing the sacrifice of Ohio Fallen Heroes. He concurred, and Senate Bill 248 was introduced which created the Ohio Medal of Distinction. Over the course of the next two years, I cautiously and optimistically watched this process unfold. In January 2009, we received the news the bill passed and it was going to be signed into law. I had to pinch myself, because I couldn't believe I was part of a process creating legislation honoring all of Ohio's fallen heroes and their families! It was my privilege to be part of the committee to design the actual medal, and on November 10, 2010, the first medals were presented to the families of Ohio's finest. Watching each family walk across the stage to receive their loved one's award warmed my heart, and I knew this was the first of many award ceremonies.

With God's guidance, we have a public platform to speak for those who cannot—and, because of that platform I am invited to tell our story, speak out for our returning veterans, and bring to the surface the struggles of the Gold Star families. But, I didn't realize when I started this process it would take a toll on my family. Unintentionally, I focused my life on my dead son, and I didn't realize how much I ignored my wife and living sons. My inattentiveness caused my children to live in the shadow of their hero brother, and I learned the hard way when you're going through grief, it's easy to be oblivious to the needs of those you love. I didn't realize grief overcomes common sense, and my grief was my focal point.

I didn't realize my grief *wasn't* worse than everybody else's …

13

Fractures

Reality. We knew our lives were different, because the world didn't stop. I knew we had to move forward—but, to be honest I didn't have a clue how to do it. When we welcomed in the 2007 New Year, I prayed to God the year would be better than the previous one—I wanted to believe it, but I knew it probably wouldn't be so. I also knew I wasn't prepared for the myriad changes that accompany a bereaved parent trying to function within a bereaved family.

As difficult as it was, Melissa returned to work, and I returned to my company with hope our lives would return to normal—we craved normalcy, but it proved elusive, and it didn't happen. Everything kept coming at us—nothing was easy, nothing was normal. Our once vibrant home was cloaked in silence—no music, no laughter, and our family resembled four little islands. We were dealing with grief in our own ways, and it was especially difficult for me because, as a Dad, we're fixers. But, I couldn't do anything to fix my family, or myself. The best I could do was to try to be ahead of the game, and I'm certain I didn't do that very well. Knowing I couldn't fix … us … I tried to be strong. In time, however, the numbing aspect of grief waned and pain surfaced, staking its claim on my life.

That's when I began to feel out of balance. I tried desperately to hold on, but after eighteen months, I spiraled downward. There were pressures at home and work, and one of my coworkers knew I was struggling without Heath in my life. She said the real issue was I needed balance. *What?* There's no such thing as balance in a situation such as this! Everything was out of control, and, nothing—*nothing*—felt right. Coworkers didn't handle the situation well, and they chose to deal with it callously. I was a bit surprised at their lack of compassion, and I found myself not wanting to be around them, or anyone like them. I needed allies who would support, and encourage me.

Unfortunately, there were few—except for family and friends, of course. And, with my behavior, I wasn't sure how long they'd be around.

Loneliness saturated everything. I never thought I would be as lonely as I was—and, am—and I never thought I would be as lost. Loneliness was my constant companion, and it embedded itself in my soul. I couldn't find the intimacy in relationships I used to have, and I still struggle with it. Spilling my guts to a counselor helped as I continued my efforts to get a grip, and he pointed out because I'm visible to the public and around many people, doesn't mean they're my friends. He's right. I view them as acquaintances, or business associates.

I hated weekends—still do—because they provide too much time to feel, and think. I didn't do anything, or go anywhere, and all I wanted to do was sleep away those endless days. My therapist prescribed an antidepressant, and it quickly became my best friend—I could drop off into a dreamless sleep, and the pain would recede.

Unintentionally, I withdrew from Melissa—I got home from work emotionally drained, trudged upstairs to our bedroom, hit the sack, and hibernated there for the rest of the night. My man cave. I was obsessed with my dead son—and everything I thought, or did, was with Heath in mind. I didn't realize there's a fine line between memorializing and enshrining him, and lack of that realization destroyed me.

Fractures

Melissa didn't deal with life well after Heath's death—my neglecting her ticked her off, and with good reason. My life was one of excessive drinking and abusing my meds, and one evening I passed out in a chair in our family room. I came to for a second, only to realize she was screaming and throwing things at me. Even after that, I couldn't get it together enough to function as a husband, and a parent.

Everything changed for Melissa, and she halted her life to focus on Chandler and Ashton twenty-four seven. During the thick of it, Melissa pressed on while I immersed myself in booze and prescription meds.

And, self-pity.

There was no doubt—I was self-focused. I thought my grief was greater than hers, and, therefore, my grief trumped hers. It took me a long time to realize all of us were grieving, and in pain. And that pain was so unbearable, so palpable, I wasn't capable of helping them.

Again, I was falling apart.

But, this time, I hit rock bottom. The pressures of work, and the devastating shock of Heath's death were wearing me out at an alarming rate. I lost weight, and my anxiety warped into hyper-drive. I knew my visits to our family doctor weren't going to cut it because my behavior was beyond his ability to treat me. It wasn't that he didn't try—but I traveled down such a dark road, both of us realized I needed a different type of medical professional.

The mental health type.

Admittedly, I'm a bit on the fence about counseling—I tried it, but with mixed results. It helped me make better decisions, but it didn't relieve the pain. One counselor, however, had a peculiar way of helping me deal with my anger—she had me write down the names of people and things making me angry—not on a piece of paper, though—on eggs! Then she took me out to a field, and instructed me to throw the eggs. At first, I wasn't too successful—turns out I wasn't targeting the right focus points of my anger. That is, until I began thinking about what happened soon after President Bush left office. I wrote the former president and thanked him for his service to the country, and I told him of Heath's death. I'm not sure what I expected from him, but I do know a mass-produced photo of his inauguration wasn't it. No signature. No letter. No *I'm sorry to learn of Heath's death*. Nothing. I thought this was a colossal slap in the face, and I was furious about how my son's Commander in Chief thanked him for his service.

The good news is the eggs worked! I took the picture of the inauguration, and I threw eggs at it as hard as I could, screaming all the while. It wasn't a huge success for diminishing my anger, but it was a success!

The stress of everything from the military, media attention, and George W.'s snub took its toll on my family's life. We tapped the reset button on our grieving processes and, as the boys grew older, they began to re-process their brother's death, understanding it from a new perspective. For Chandler, it was more difficult to live under the shadow of his fallen brother, and his heroism. I know my actions were unacceptable, but it was nearly impossible to remember I had to be there for my living children, too. No excuses—just observation. I was oblivious to everything other than my personal grief, and pain.

I didn't know how to deal with this new stranger in my life—the anger—so I asked God to help me. I'm not sure what I expected, but what I got didn't really help at all. Every facet of my life was slow, long, and hard, and I needed God to take away the external things that were smothering me—work, situations with the boys—and I think that was when I began to experience consuming loneliness. I tried to connect with God, but it didn't happen. During the first couple of years following Heath's death, I found myself remembering a new anniversary. On the twenty-second of each month, I relived the events of November 22nd, and soul-slicing pain surged through every part of my being. I was beyond distraught. Beyond angry. Beyond disbelief. Physical and mental changes emerged—weight loss, loss of sleep, no sex drive, and the inability to continue personal relationships. I felt as if my demons were encircling me and, as a grieving father, I knew I should take the lead by guiding my family through the crisis. But all I could do was grieve with total disregard for anyone else.

Each day presented new challenges—family, work, relationships, money, news of soldiers' deaths, and the on-going war. No matter how hard I tried, I couldn't run or hide.

———————

My heart is pierced, and its wound refuses to heal. My therapist tells me the wounds don't go away—I know I'm going to be lonely and sad, but it's what I do with loneliness and sadness that makes a difference.

Grieving parents are mired in their anger, and they never let it go—it's so easy to become trapped in the totality of being a bereaved parent. By writing this book, I want people who read it to know I was screwed up. My professional life fell apart, and I lost friends. However, I'm finally moving forward with dignity and courage.

Fractures

I'm still struggling, but, with time, I'm becoming healthier, and I'm trying to maintain a positive mental attitude. But there are constant reminders forcing my memories to the surface and I, once again, relive the days and years of our grief. When Bin Laden was killed, it were as if a scab were ripped from my skin. Heath's mission was to find Bin Laden, and I rejoiced with the rest of our country when I heard the news. I quickly sobered, however, when I considered my son gave his life for an effort that was eventually successful.

Throughout the years of our acceptance and recovery from paralyzing grief, I didn't realize how much time and energy I spent defending Heath's death. Everywhere I went, people commented our soldiers were dying in vain, and my emotional energy was depleted simply because I was constantly defending why my son died. I can't accept his fight for the safety of our country was a waste. I refuse to accept it. In my view, Bin Laden's death validated Heath. Other Gold Star families and I never thought we'd hear such vindicating news, and we were caught off guard. Even though the news was good, it was another reality slap—the war is still real, my son is still dead, but the person responsible no longer threatens our country.

I cried for days after learning of Bin Laden's death—it were as if I were reliving the initial days after Heath's death. Melissa and I received texts, phone calls, and Facebook messages thanking us for our sacrifice and Heath's contribution to this very important moment in our nation's history.

So, the task for me was to figure out how I could forgive everyone involved in my son's death. A bucket list seemed like a good idea, so I jotted down random thoughts, and random personal goals. I figured if I could achieve personal goals, then perhaps they could free me from my oppressive grief. First on my list? I want to go to Iraq. I want to meet the people of Iraq, and see for myself that my son's life made a difference. If I can do that, I believe it will help me forgive, and, in a concrete way, I will see something positive.

My depression increased, and my situation at work was abysmal. I felt hopeless, and my downward spiral amplified my wanting to abuse alcohol, and my prescription meds. Thoughts of suicide tangled in my brain, and I thought about how good it would feel to feel nothing. No grief. No pain. Of course, I didn't really want to kill myself, but I didn't want to wake up either—I just wanted to sleep my life away.

Fractures

The first time I took a handful of pills, I looked at them and thought, *what the hell?* They felt sticky and dry in my mouth, and as I washed them down with a gulp of water, I wasn't sure if I would wake up—and I didn't care.

I don't remember too much about my suicide attempt, but the reality is I should have been hospitalized long before I decided to do myself in. Chandler begged Melissa to take me to the hospital, but she didn't understand mental health issues, and she thought I would be stigmatized once people found out I couldn't cope.

And so it was. My pivotal point.

The depression continued, but after the episode with the pills, I knew I had to make some changes in my life. I came to realize that, sometimes, Gold Star parents are put in positions we shouldn't be in—there's a public side to being a Gold Star family, and we have to negotiate it with dignity. It became apparent our grief was public grief, but our pain was private. We learned how to present ourselves in public in a manner that maintained our dignity, but the reality of our private lives was escalating pain.

It didn't help any the war went on for so long—when a local service member was killed, we wanted to support the fallen trooper's family, but it was too painful. We adopted a 'reach out later' perspective because every time we went to a memorial service, it were as if we picked off another scab.

Family members had a difficult time understanding the depth of our grief, and after attending a memorial service in Columbus for Ohio's fallen heroes, my brother asked, "How do you do this?" He was shaken physically and emotionally.

"Welcome to my reality. It's hard as hell. What do you do when people are honoring your son?"

What we did was live each day at a time, and we learned how to be selective regarding which events we chose to attend. Some people understood what we were going through, and others chose to stick their heads in the sand. Work became unbearable, and my depression prevented me from being as productive as possible. I didn't know that under the American Disabilities Act (ADA) depression was a protected class or a protected group, and it wasn't until I enrolled in a Business Law course I learned my depression is considered a disability. I discussed my situation with my Business Law prof, and she indicated my employer was trying to get rid of me. She also gave me tips about how to handle the situation, and I felt for the first time in many months I was gaining a modicum of control.

That was the beginning of my setting boundaries. When my supervisor stepped over the line—again—I told her I was reporting her behavior to Human Resources. However, no matter how I attempted to diffuse an ugly, contentious situation, it continued to escalate. It did do one thing for me, however—I learned to say no.

I learned to take back control.

On November 22, 2006, my life was over in an instant—it changed in a flash, and it changed forever. I questioned everything, and Heath's death changed me—it also changed how I perceived and dealt with my family, my presuppositions about politics, and my Christian faith. Most of all, I questioned what's important in life. *Things? People? Ideas? Family? Work?* Before Heath's death, I devoted myself to my career, and I realized I missed so much because my job was always first on my list of priorities—I regret that. I didn't realize my priorities were skewed, and it took a catastrophic event to stop me cold. Now I consider it a blessing. It's almost as if God were saying, "Okay. I'm giving you a clean slate to live your life again. What will you differently?"

I had to think about that …

I prayed to God to help me make my life purposeful, and I could feel Heath's short life was guiding me to be purposeful. He knew the cost of what he was going to do—he knew the reality and, in the end, he was very courageous.

He did what God called him to do.

I couldn't say the same.

Heath inspired me to want to live a purposeful life—not a life of merely surviving the day-to-day business. As I said, my loneliness was created by my lack of intimacy in relationships, as well as my inability to be transparent and real. I quickly learned people wear down with depression, and it was difficult to find people who wouldn't judge me.

I turned, again, to my relationship with God. I began attending Mass daily and I began to meditate, keep a journal, and pray—for my family, and Heath—and I reconnected with God, feeling His presence in my heart. One thing I like about the Catholic Church is we remember those who have gone before us—they're part of the Communion of Saints. They're active and alive and, in my belief, Heath is up in Heaven cheering us on. I believe Heath actively intercedes for us on behalf of Christ.

There's power in that.

In January 2008, we traveled to St. Patrick's Cathedral in New York City, and I felt as if God were tugging at my heart, prodding me to come home.

The following month we attended Mass with another Gold Star family, and while I sat in the quietude of the Sanctuary, God said, "This is your home. This is where I want you to be."

Since then, I haven't looked back, and my faith is a very important part of this journey. I still consider myself fractured, and I still feel a general level of sadness. I still carry a level of depression ... and that's where the concept of 'redemptive suffering' comes in. *Life is hard, so how can I endure the pain, and use it for the greater good?*

By the way, I used my newfound faith to take control of my life, and I sued my employer. My case is ongoing in Federal Court ...

14

Desecration of Honor

On June 10, 2010, I received a call from a reporter.

"Mr. Warner, can I get a comment from you about the report released today regarding Arlington National Cemetery?"

I had no idea what he was talking about …

"Let me get back to you—I'm busy at the moment. I'll call you back in about fifteen minutes." I was caught off guard, and I didn't want to offer any comments without having time to think first.

What now? I immediately called one of my friends whose brother is buried at Arlington—she also worked in public relations for a nonprofit organization in Washington D.C., and I knew if anyone knew the details, she would.

She told me there was a Congressional investigation regarding Arlington Administation abuses, and mismarked graves—the remains of at least two hundred soldiers purportedly buried in the cemetery may have been misidentified or misplaced. Her words made my skin crawl as I envisioned the shadow creeping over America's sacred ground.

All I could think about was Heath.

I was relieved when she told me it didn't affect Section 60—thank God, because that was the last thing I needed on my plate. It did bring to mind, though, a blurb I heard on TV about unidentifiable remains at Arlington, but I chalked it up to rumor.

True to my word, I spoke with the reporter who called earlier.

"We assume it's an isolated incident, and we aren't concerned at this point." Little did I know how this investigation at Arlington National Cemetery was going to flip my world upside down.

My dissatisfaction with Arlington started prior to the allegations of administrative abuse, because when we buried Heath, we believed burying him at Arlington was the ultimate honor we could give him. Please understand—there's a tradeoff with burying a soldier at Arlington, because it's a public and tourist attraction. Choosing to bury Heath at Arlington meant we'd lose a sense of privacy when visiting Heath's grave, and the more time we spent there, concerns slowly percolated to the surface. Lack of privacy morphed into an intense invasion of privacy, because Arlington Administration wouldn't contact us regarding special events scheduled at the cemetery. For example, Arlington failed to notify us of its embedding a production crew for a three-month shoot for a special on families of fallen soldiers. On one of our visits, we traveled six hours only to be greeted by a videographer the second we stepped out of the car. Another family ambled by, and the woman commented, "It's okay—they're here with HBO." It struck me odd because she was equipped with a lapel microphone—when she spoke to us, she was recording! The ambling family was clearly a setup, and staged for the benefit of the camera.

We were mortified, angry, and disappointed—time we were planning to spend with Heath was ruined.

The following day I sat down with the producer, and we chatted for about an hour. After our conversation, I felt the project was worthwhile, and I signed a release giving our permission to include our video and statements in the project. I felt the greater good of the project was to educate people about

Gold Star families, and the lonely journey we walk in our grieving process.

Another thing that bothered me about Arlington was Section 60 was the final resting ground for fallen soldiers of the Iraq and Afghanistan wars. It was a circus environment and a destination visit for gawking tourists—unless we arrived early or late, there wasn't any privacy.

The Arlington Visitors' Center resembles a museum, and it buzzed with tourists—the fact it's a working cemetery somehow was lost.

Clearly, it's a business.

Section 60 is one of the top visitor attractions, but unlike the Tomb of the Unknown Soldier and John F. Kennedy's grave, there isn't anyone monitoring the level of chatter. There isn't anyone advising visitors to be respectful.

In May of 2010, I attended a TAPS conference and while there, I jogged from Crystal City to Heath's grave at Arlington. I couldn't believe what I saw as I passed the Visitors' Center—a group of adults having its picture taken at the main sign—a woman lying on the ground, her head propped up by her elbow, two other women provocatively stood at her side, and the rest of the pack hovered around the sign. *Really?* Are we at the amusement park? It was clear that Section 60 was crowded with Memorial Day weekend visitors.

I videotaped the circus-like atmosphere on my cell phone, and showed it to a Cleveland reporter friend of mine because I wanted to show what was going on in Arlington—and this was *before* I knew the magnitude of Arlington's administrative ineptitude! I was already a pressure cooker as I attempted to deal with my anger issues, and I started to simmer each time I thought about the cemetery. I quickly learned, though, my instincts were correct— behind the scenes at Arlington an unbelievable disaster festered, and it was about to seep into the hearts of those who were the parents, and families of fallen soldiers.

The reporter clued me in about Arlington's problems and I wasn't too concerned, but on top of what I was already feeling, I think I'm accurate in saying I was edgy. But, I had to back burner the whole thing because I had to deal with the drama at work.

I wasn't doing well.

Shortly after we received a phone call in July informing us the investigation expanded to over six thousand graves, a different reporter contacted us about Arlington's disgusting mess. He filled me in, and I was stunned to learn the cemetery wasn't computerized, and that it was using an archaic system.

And then everything exploded.

We called the 800 number for verification, and we received a call in August. The monotone voice read an inadequately prepared statement, and I requested a copy of the document for our records.

When I received the document, my blood pressure spiked when I noticed serious flaws in the paperwork. Information was missing, incomplete, or incorrect, and it took me about two seconds to place a call to Katherine Condon, Executive Director of Arlington National Cemetery. I told her I was concerned about the inaccuracy of the report, and I wanted to be certain about where my son was buried. Initially, she seemed passionate about restoring the dignity of Arlington, and I offered to be part of the solution to the problem.

Although Katherine committed to contacting me on Friday, I didn't hear from her until the following Wednesday.

"I have information for you—your son was kept at a local funeral home in Falls Church."

"How do you know?"

"It's the contracted funeral home Arlington always uses."

Hmmm. I told her I was with friends, and I needed to call her the following day. After we hung up, I contacted my florist in D.C., and I asked her to make a call to the funeral home to verify if it received a call from the cemetery. She was familiar with the funeral home, and she promptly granted my request.

I find it odd Arlington *and* the funeral home operated their respective businesses without being computerized. The funeral home did search, but they couldn't locate any records of Heath's being at their funeral home—ever.

The first lie.

The following morning, I participated in a conference call with Katherine and the Arlington Superintendent, Patrick Hallinan. I asked her to review the information she told me the previous evening with the superintendent, and she simply reiterated what she told me.

"Why do you have Arlington listed as the final funeral home? Why wasn't the funeral home on there, or Heitger's?"

Katherine explained there must be an error.

"Will you please fax me the paperwork?" I figured she didn't have any paperwork, and her response confirmed my suspicions.

"Mr. Warner, I don't have any paperwork. I thought my word was good enough." Talk about a pressure cooker moment!

"Perhaps you don't understand the significance of this. There's a material flaw regarding the record keeping of those who are buried in Arlington

National Cemetery, and that's why we're at this point." I waited for a response.

Silence.

"Well, I wasn't aware you wanted the paperwork, but I will have it for you on Friday."

Of course the paperwork never came. The only piece of paperwork I received a year later was a bill of lading for when Heath's body was received at the airport. If there were additional paperwork, it was gone. Destroyed by a flood.

Or, so I was told.

That's when it became adversarial between Katherine and me. We had no other choice but to decide to move forward with a disinterment, and I formally requested Katherine to make the arrangements. She complied, and the disinterment was scheduled for Wednesday, September 15, 2010, at eight o'clock in the morning.

I forgot to tell you ... in July 2010, I spent some time at St. Patrick's Cathedral in New York City, and it was there I was gifted with a clear message from God:

You're going to do what I want you to do. You're going to speak. Listen to Me ...

I had no idea what He was talking about, but I wrote it in my journal. Shortly after was the Arlington crisis, and I found myself in the national spotlight, dealing with a crisis situation—I didn't know what to do, or how to do it.

September 15th dawned sunny and clear, and, after a restless night, we arrived at the cemetery for the disinterment. My brother was there to video the process, and we requested a priest to be present, as well. Chugging and belching heavy equipment was already in place, and we knew they prepared the previous evening for the casket to be lifted that morning. Katherine was there, along with an Arlington higher up, as well as several Arlington workers.

The disinterment procedure began promptly at eight, and we watched as workers hooked heavy chains to Heath's casket to lift it from the ground. It was immediately clear the workers were struggling with something, but because we were standing several feet away, I couldn't clearly see what was happening.

As the casket rose from the earth, it tilted precariously—we could see its seal was broken, and a top portion of the casket lid was creased and opened. As the casket tipped, gallons of water gushed from the inside of Heath's casket—his remains sliding forward, and slipping through the open lid.

Melissa's and my horror was inexplicable! We watched as our son's remains oozed from his casket, and it was clear the damage to the casket occurred the evening before, and that's why the workers were taking so long to raise it. Twenty minutes passed as we waited, and we were informed there was a water problem—a water table problem, to be exact.

But ... we were told they only excavated the gravesite the evening before—we knew they must have disinterred him the night before because there were gallons of water *in* his casket.

We knew.

"Liars!" Melissa screamed, and I knew I had to be strong for her. I held her tightly to give her strength, and my sister, Valerie, held me tightly. I wanted to run over to Condon and Hallihan, who were standing stiff and emotionless, and throw them into Heath's grave. Not that I would actually do it, of course, but my anger was over the top.

Naturally, the Arlington reps said the casket popped open on the way up that morning—a rather poor attempt at spin control, don't you think?

So there is was—the second lie. Melissa and I were keenly aware of what was taking place. Heath's casket was completely rusted, and it looked as if it had been in the ground for a hundred years—I couldn't believe what I was seeing, or experiencing! The crazy thing was God was right there with me! He whispered this prayer in my ear:

*Christ be with me. Christ before me. Christ
behind me. Christ in me. Christ on my right. Christ
on my left. Christ where I lie. Christ where I sit.
Christ where I arise.*

I knew God was my strength through everything
I was witnessing, and what was ahead of me.

I squeezed Melissa's hand to let her know I was
right there. Sobbing, we watched as workers loaded
our son's casket onto a truck that would take it to a
separate building for proper identification. We were
barely cognizant of the priest's blessings as the
casket emerged and was placed on the truck—our
horror was so overwhelming, we were at a complete
loss for words.

Finally loaded with its precious cargo, the truck
accelerated slowly, and deliberately made its way
from the gravesite to a small building where the
identification would take place.

The truck transported Heath's remains to Echo
Building 123, which was nothing more than a mere
garage. Originally, they were to transport him to a
local funeral home but, at the last minute,
Superintendent Hallihan informed us they were

going to perform the physical identification onsite. I assumed they had a proper mortuary facility to handle this process—boy, was I wrong!

Brendan, a military brother of Heath's, offered to make the identification.

"I don't want Mrs. Warner and you to see him," he said. His offer was heartwarming, and I appreciated his wanting, and needing, to be a part of the process. We nodded our consent, and I gave him a picture of the tattoo on Heath's arm the Heitgers took in Canton, and he started toward the building.

I hadn't planned to go inside, but in light of what we just witnessed, and what we'd gone through, something inside me told me Heath's friend should not go in alone. At the last minute I yelled for him to wait, and we entered the garage together.

As I stepped inside, I noticed a brand new silver and chrome casket. It struck me odd because Katherine Condon said they would simply open the casket, we would identify his tattoo, they would close the lid, and rebury him in his original casket.

The flatbed truck with Heath's casket on it was to the far right, and the funeral director was using a five-foot long winch in an effort to open the rusted seal of the bottom half of the casket. Once opened, Heath's dog tags must have been visible, for Superintendent Hallihan brought them to me. The funeral director jumped off the truck, and Brendan jumped on—he looked so strong in his military dress blues, holding the picture I gave him of the tattoo on Heath's right arm.

He just stood there, and I could see he was trembling, his head bowed. I felt his fear, and I was appalled no one offered to help him. Two Army officers, the superintendent, and the funeral director who was hiding behind a stairwell, simply left Brendan to fend for himself.

As I watched in disbelief what they were doing to this Marine, I did what I said I wouldn't do. I crossed to the side of the flatbed, climbed on the tire, and hoisted myself onto the flatbed.

Then I understood why Brendan was trembling.

I looked into Heath's casket, and before us was an ugly pile of goo. I couldn't figure out what was what, and I literally had no idea of what I was seeing. I knelt down beside his casket and, without hesitation, I slid my hand inside of it to see if I could determine what was left of Heath.

Within moments, I felt his belt buckle, pulled it out, and I asked if I could have it. One of the Army officers gingerly took it from me, and soon I found the other half, its material rotten. I couldn't be certain, but it seemed as if Heath were headless. I felt some upper torso, some leg, and what was left of his torso was on top of his arm.

"I found his arm. Get your ass up here and do your job. I want to see his arm," I barked at the funeral director. He reluctantly got back on the truck, knelt beside the casket, and tried to shift Heath's remains, gagging the whole time. Suddenly his torso shifted, and in some bizarre, weird way, that pile of goo became Heath to me again. I made sense of his form, and as I was still kneeling, I began to wipe away mud that was on his arm. His casket was loaded with mud, and as I wiped it away, I realized the only part of him that hadn't decomposed was his right arm—it was the only identifiable part of Heath. I have Heitger's Funeral Services to thank for that—they prepared Heath's right arm for viewing four years previously, and the excellence of their work showed.

The Army officer handed me a handkerchief to wipe the mud from Heath's arm, and it was then I heard God. *Why are you crying, Scott? Look, Heath's gone. Heath's gone. He's with me. He's complete again. What you're looking at isn't Heath, anymore. He's gone.*

There wasn't any doubt the remains in that broken, soggy, destroyed casket were my boy.

Handing me a pair of latex gloves, an Army officer asked me to remove my gloves and place them in the hazardous waste bag. The same with my fedora and jacket. As I stripped the gloves from my hand, I felt excited because I knew it was Heath—but I had no idea what the experience would do to me emotionally. It was one of the worst things imaginable, and as soon as I identified our son, they ushered me from the building. It was plain to me that something terribly wrong just took place—no parent, let alone a bereaved parent, should be in such a position. Our human nature isn't equipped to see, or do, the things I experienced.

The Marine funeral director told us he was taking over—he took Heath's remains, and placed them in the brand new casket in the garage. He completely covered Heath with blankets and towels, so the only thing visible was Heath's tattoo. Then, he covered Heath with a new casket blanket. When he finished preparing Heath for us to view, Melissa and I entered the garage with the Marine funeral director.

Once I left the building, I was on adrenaline, and I couldn't believe what I just experienced.

"Melissa! You aren't going to believe what happened in the garage." As I shared the story, she was horrified and began to cry, and after a few moments, the Marine funeral director escorted Melissa and me back inside.

I know it was difficult for her, because she had an unrealistic and idyllic picture in her mind of Heath resting peacefully. It comforted her, and to realize he was gone and decomposing was something no mother should have to endure.

As she prepared herself, I told her everything was okay and she could handle it. The Marine was comforting her, and he lifted the blanket so she could clearly see his arm. She looked at it briefly, her sobs soft and surging.

"Okay—that's enough." The strong chemical odor used to stop decomposition assaulted us, and even within the short period of time it took to identify his remains, Heath's arm was already beginning to turn black.

With dignity, the Marine lowered the blanket, and he arranged several things on its lower half—there was a black felt small bag containing the cleaned up belt buckle, a bag containing Heath's rusted dog tags, and a time capsule for which we could write a note—then it would be screwed into the end of the casket. Melissa wrote a brief note, and the Marine handed us new dog tags—there was also a set to attach to the end of the casket, and another to place inside.

I had to compose myself, so I asked if I could have some time alone. Brendan took charge of Melissa, found her a tissue, and gently guided her outside. I asked for the priest, and I felt for him—he was in the middle of this, and it took him about fifteen minutes to muster his courage based on what he witnessed at the gravesite.

A friend of mine gave me a special rosary with St. Padre Peo on it, and with that rosary the priest blessed Heath with the sign of the cross, and we prayed together. Then the Marine master sergeant came in, and asked if we were ready to leave.

We were—we accomplished what we had to do, and we were ready to proceed with the burial. One of the contentions we had with Arlington was Heath's re-burial, so I asked if he were to be buried with any honors.

"No, he's already received his honors," Katherine Condon answered matter-of-factly. But the Marine told me he was going to take care of the honors, and when Heath's casket arrived at the cemetery plot, it was draped with a flag, and the Marine honor guard was present. They carried him to the grave, performed the final salute by raising the casket above their heads, and they slowly placed it on the ground. I brought Heath's white dress hat with me, and I gave it to Brendan, asking him to lay it on top of the casket. He did, and he saluted Heath.

And then it was over—desecration was replaced with honor. I brought six long-stemmed roses, and I gave one to each of my siblings who were there with us, and one to Brendan, as well. We placed them on his casket, and we paid our respects. Our friends who lived in the area came to support us and shower us with love, and somehow—somehow—we managed to finish the ceremony more shaken than we thought possible.

The Marines folded the flag, and instead of handing it to Melissa, they gave it to me. It was very different from the first time we buried Heath, because the first time we buried him we were so numb, we couldn't feel it.

This time we could.

15

A Complicated Journey to Healing

It came as no surprise that I suffered with Post
Traumatic Stress Disorder (PTSD), and I found
trying to keep Heath alive was harder than letting
him go. It was harder than saying goodbye, and I
was emotionally drained and physically tired.

I was worn out.

Part of PTSD is avoiding the pain, so I
immersed myself in activities and wound up
alienating myself from my family, and I didn't deal
with my emotional issues. I often retreated to the
man cave, and I quickly discovered the five stages of
grieving was a bunch of crap. Instead, I adopted
what I call 'catastrophic craziness'—I had to manage
the best I could while my life continued to spiral out
of control. I figured out there are different types of
losses, so when my supervisor at work told me 'a

loss is a loss', she didn't know what she was talking about. Dealing with Heath's death was, and is, challenging—it's because the nature and trauma associated with his death took grieving to a different, higher level. It was then I tried to figure out what was going on. But, no matter how I tried, I didn't understand it—it was too big, and I couldn't get my arms around it.

I think I exhibited each symptom associated with PTSD—avoidance, keeping busy, obsessed with the dead, and isolation. I spent too much time by myself, avoiding people. We were a military family, we lost our son in the war, and no one seemed to care because their lives went on as usual.

Sleep still eludes me, and my mind wrestles each night with memories of my son. To ease my constant, running thoughts, I take a regimen of meds for anxiety, depression, and sleeping. I can't function without them, and they allow me to maintain a pace with which I can function. Recurring dreams of Heath's death, the explosion, his body exploded and torn apart, haunt me incessantly—I feel guilty because Heath died alone, depressed, and sad. I didn't know Heath was depressed until I spoke with one of his military brothers who told me Heath was having a difficult time coping. I also spoke to one of his superiors, and I asked him about Heath's depression—he confirmed Heath was very homesick and demoted in rank because he fell asleep at his post. He punished Heath, and he felt guilty about that.

"It's time you quit beating yourself up. You were at war, you crawled up to that post, and Heath was on the floor. You thought he was dead! As a leader, you did your best. Let it go. I forgive you." I'm not sure my forgiveness relieved his guilt, but it felt good to overcome one of my demons—I had to begin forgiving those whom I believed contributed to my son's death.

Over the years, Heath's platoon friends filled in the blanks about Heath's death—they told us his death was caused by a poor decision made by his Commanding Officer. His C.O. ordered his regiment to return to an unsecured area—an area in which there was terrorist activity. There was a general understanding troops had to be careful by changing traffic paths, and Heath's C.O. ordered them to take the same path, and turn around at the same point— and, the regiment followed those orders seven days in a row. The other Marines tried to talk to him about it because it was dangerous to the patrol, but he was stubborn, and ordered them into the path of danger anyway.

I asked for a report of Heath's death because whenever there's a kill, the military has to verify it's a legitimate kill. However, no report existed for

A Complicated Journey to Healing

Heath's—I only know it to be true because I was told the same story by three or four members of Heath's unit. In fact, when Heath was in training, he told me his Commanding Officer was fresh out of school, and they called him Pretty Boy.

"He's a nice guy," he said, "but he has no field experience. Dad, this guy is going to get me killed."

I didn't know then it was an unforgiving prophecy.

And that's part of my forgiveness issue—I can't find it in myself to forgive. I know I have to, but there are so many levels of forgiveness, it's hard to get my arms around it. How do I forgive our former president, our politicians, Bin Laden and his terrorist plots, the American people who put their heads in the sand, the Commanding Officer, Melissa, and me—how do I forgive all of them? Where should I draw the line? My family was the victim of a sham investigation, and insulted by convenient lies intended to rewrite the story.

And that's why I want to share my *entire* story—now it's under the Freedom of Information Act, and you have access to all of this information.

All according to God's message that day at St. Pat's …

I found my voice.

16

Have Faith, Keep Talking

Not too long ago, I interviewed a WWII survivor and, during the interview, I asked him what words of encouragement he had for returning vets.

"Have faith, keep talking." He went on to explain that having faith in God and finding the ability to forgive, facilitate finding peace. Keep talking, because if emotions are buried, there is more pain—I'm a living testament to that!

I knew I had to focus on Melissa and our relationship, and I knew we needed to forgive each other. It's been a tough go, but the cool thing is we're falling in love again! Pain drove us apart, and pain is driving us back to love. And part of our falling in love again was finding God—again. We began praying and finding God together, asking Him for His forgiveness. We began rediscovering God's love, our love for each other, and He gave us strength by answering our prayers.

––––––––––––––

The upshot of all of this is I had to learn how to negotiate with a society that doesn't understand. It's only through talking and writing this book that people are going to understand what Gold Star families endure. I've had people say to me, "Things must come so easy for you—you have such a nice house." Not true. What this war has done to my family and children will always be a destructive force, and it creates a void—unless we fight and work against it.

When Melissa and I went to Arlington for the disinterment, my employer took the position we went on a vacation to Washington, D.C., and I was clawing through his casket like a crazy person. That's why I appeared on CNN to tell the public I was lied to, why my trust was broken, and why I was left with no options.

Shortly after that appearance, I received a letter from a man in North Carolina in which he commented what I did at Arlington will be remembered as a great act of love. He also told me I did what I needed to do for my family because now we will never have to wonder *what if?* A man I don't know applauded my courage and strength, and he affirmed I'll always be remembered for that love.

I have to admit ... on days when I'm down about Arlington, second-guessing why I did what I did, I read his kind words, and I find them to be a tremendous blessing.

Before November 22, 2006, my life was defined one way, and after that day, it was defined in a new way. So many questions—*who is Scott Warner? What are my passions? What's important? What are my priorities?*

Nearly six years later, Melissa and I finally found professionals at the new Vet Center located in our community who could really help us. The purpose of the Vet Center is to provide counseling, and bereavement counseling services to returning veterans, their families, and Gold Star Families in order to help them re-integrate into the civilian world. My counselor is a degreed therapist who is a Vietnam veteran and, to this day, suffers with PTSD. Heath's death nearly destroyed our family, and we needed help to bring healing to us, individually, and to our family.

"You two are an amazing couple—most people in your situation never make it to these chairs," he commented. And as we talked, it was clear Melissa and I are still best friends, and in love. After that appointment, both of us had a new sense of hope our marriage will survive.

We're in the process of de-shrining, and we'll keep only a couple of things that are fun memories of Heath. We're replacing them with home decorations normal people put up. I guess we're regaining our sense of family—thank God we found professionals who can help Melissa and me get through it.

Since Heath's death, I am emerging bold and courageous. I ran two marathons, I'm a Civil Service Commissioner for our city, an author, and public speaker. I learned how to be an advocate for surviving military families, returning veterans, and individuals with mental health issues by using a new platform for my voice. I'm an actor in community theatre, and I'm having a blast! Most important, I'm becoming the husband, and father I am supposed to be.

Heath is—and, will be forever—in our hearts, but the reality is we need to live for the living.

That's what Heath would want for us.

There are various reasons I was compelled to write this book—first, I believe God put this in my heart, so Melissa and I can help other hurting families. Second, I want to educate the public about the long-term consequences of war. I hate war. I hate what it does to individuals, families, and to our world.

Last, I wrote this book to honor a hero, and remember my son, Heath. Before Heath left for war, he shared with us he wanted to write a book about his life. He wanted other young people to know one person can make a difference in this world, and each person needs to follow passionately his or her dreams.

Heath's life continues to touch thousands of lives throughout the world—he was conceived in pain, and his life ended in pain. He unexpectedly came into this world, and he left it unexpectedly. Somewhere in between, however, there is a great story of love, forgiveness, and redemption.

This one's for you, Kiddo!

Love, your proud Gold Star father.

Fast forward. June, 2012. I was on my last mile of the Canton Marathon—uphill, and a long, steep incline. The more I pushed, the more my legs cramped. The finish line was at the Pro Football Hall of Fame, and by the time I reached the field, I was ready to stop running, and start walking. I caught Melissa from the corner of my eye, ducking underneath the security tape—she grabbed my hand, and said, "Oh, no, Scott, you're running to the end!" She grabbed my hand, and we ran across the finish line holding hands.

Does it get any better than that?

My dream is Melissa and I will finish this dream of life, hand-in-hand until the end, with our family beside us.

For better, or for worse, until death do us part.

In Memoriam

The following is a 9/11 tribute I wrote in 2007, and it captures what I felt in my heart. I share this each year as my way of reflecting on the tragic events of 9/11 that forever changed my family's lives.

I hope it touches you in a special way …

9/11 Remembered

I remember 9/11 so vividly. The drive into work was picture perfect. I remember thinking what an awesome early fall day—sunny, warm, and the sky was brilliant blue. As I sat at my desk with the radio on, I heard the announcer break in that a plane had crashed into the World Trade Centers.

I remember on 9/11 thinking maybe there was fog, and a small Cessna had, unfortunately, lost course and crashed. Shortly thereafter, as a news reporter was interviewing an eyewitness, there were screams as the second plane crashed into the second tower.

Then, everything seemed to stop.

Could it be terrorist? My employer sent us home, and we were glued to the TV as the drama unfolded. Little did I know that not only did the world change that day, but how dramatically and intimately it would change my family, and life.

I remember on 9/11, that my son, Heath, would say he was going to fight for his country. I did not know then he would lose his life fighting a war so his family could have a safer future.

I remember 9/11 as the day he left to travel to this foreign field of battle, and it would be the last day he would be alive on American soil. A day of last phone texts, last phone calls, and the day I began to worry endlessly about a son going to war.

I remember 9/11 as a bittersweet time of fond, last memories, and of the beginning of long-term pain and heartache.

I remember on 9/11, all the lives lost, the destruction, the end of a way of life America had known.

On 9/11, I pray God will be with all the families who lost their special loved ones that day, and with all the families of the brave men and women who lost their lives fighting for our national security, and freedom since then. May God give wisdom to our leaders who will ultimately lead us to a safer, free world.

God bless America, God bless you, and may God bless our men, and women, serving our country.

~ Scott Warner

ACKNOWLEDGEMENTS

CHRYSALIS PUBLISHING AUTHOR SERVICES
EDITOR: L.A. O'Neil

COVER ART DESIGN:
Scott Warner, Paul Hirsch, and L.A. O'Neil

FRONT COVER PHOTOGRAPH:
James Dreussi

BACK COVER PHOTOGRAPH:
Don Jones

SCOTT N. WARNER, M.B.A., M.A.P.P.
WARNER INSPIRATIONAL MEDIA
www.goldstarfather.com
www.pvtheathwarner.com

Made in the USA
San Bernardino, CA
25 February 2015